I0412011

Electro-Muse

Tools and Tips for the
Beginning Independent Author
in this Technological Age

Pen

©2014

All rights reserved
©2014 by Pen

*No part of this book may be reproduced or transmitted in
any form or by any means, electronic, physical or
mechanical, including photocopying, recording or by any
information storage and retrieval system, without permission
in writing from the author.*

ISBN-13: 978-1501037320
ISBN-10: 1501037323

This book is cat-approved.

For more information visit
www.penspen.info

Table of Contents

Introduction

Writing is a suspension of life in order to re-create life. ~John McPhee

The publishing industry has undergone drastic changes just in the last ten years. The Internet and the economy are the primary causes for these changes.

Long gone are the days an author's novel was serialized in a newspaper or magazine publication as were the works of Mark Twain, Charles Dickens, Harriett Beecher Stowe, Sir Arthur Conan Doyle and others.

Going fast are the days of traditional publishing houses leaving authors fewer opportunities for publishing success.

The time of the self-published author is here. And the time fast approaches when everyone and everything will be available via the Internet.

The path to self-publishing is easy yet complex. Access to self-publishing sites is only a click away. Preparation is a little rockier.

There will probably come a day when uploading files for publication is a simple task. For now, proper formatting is complicated and, at times, an arduous undertaking. Not everyone is technically savvy. Word can be a daunting program if you're not accustomed to using it. MOBI (for Kindle) and EPUB (other electronic devices) are the catch phrases of the day. Manually formatting for them by hand is out of the question for most people.

If you are one of those fortunate enough to be able to pay someone for their technical expertise in order to properly format your books prior to upload, splendid. By all means pay someone and save yourself the headache.

If, however, you are like most writers and on an anorexic budget, you might want to slog through all the necessary steps to prepare your books for publication. If you're not familiar with the technology, it won't be easy. It will be frustrating and time-consuming. You will want to pull out your hair, gnash your teeth and scream. Do so. You'll feel better.

Within these pages are instructions and tips for preparing files for publication, whether it is for print or electronic publication. Most everything in here is from my personal experience: lessons I've learned the hard way. I present them to you, dear reader and writer, in an effort to help soften your path to publication. Experience works best when it benefits others.

Don't allow yourself to be daunted by the technical aspects of getting your work out there. My own hesitation has delayed the publication of my own work for far too long. As you will find in the last chapter of this book – Dying to Be a Writer? – I delayed until it was almost too late. Don't make that mistake.

The truth of the matter is that once you have mastered the steps necessary to become an Independent Author, once you comprehend what goes into self-publishing your book, you won't soon forget.

Maybe someday someone else will benefit from your experience.

The Nuts and Bolts of Self-Publishing

The professional writer is an amateur who didn't quit.
~Richard Bach

Publishing in the Electronic Age

I have been following the publishing industry since the age of twelve. Subscribed to Writer's Digest Magazine with my first babysitting pay and purchased the Writer's Digest Market book annually.

Until, that is, I noticed a new trend.

For the last fifteen or so years, the publishing industry has undergone remarkable changes: They are going out of business on an almost daily basis.

It is, in part, due to the economy. Printing is a very expensive endeavor. I researched it in the 90s with the intention of printing my own books and magazines. The cost was quite staggering then, I can't imagine what it is now.

But the decline in the number of publishing houses to which an author can appeal is also due in part to the advent of the Internet. Years in the making it didn't take a minute for this little trinket to go viral.

And it has changed everything.

Who wants to carry a bulky book, magazine or newspaper when they can get what they want via Kindle or other electronic devices?

So, yes, a lot of publishing houses closed their doors.

This heats up the competition for and between writers trying to get published. (Yeah, like it wasn't hard enough already).

No one wants to represent or publish a book that isn't a sure-fire thing. Gone are the days when an agent or publisher took a chance on new talent. With sky-high printing costs, publishing houses want to be assured they will recoup what they invest.

This is understandable, but it hinders many talented writers from getting published.

So what is a writer to do?

Ironically, the very party guilty of putting publishers out of business is also an advantage for many writers looking to publish her or his work.

Writers can locate all types of ways to self-publish on the Internet. I use Createspace (www.createspace.com). It is a subsidiary of Amazon.com and your book is immediately available through that outlet.

Which is another sad side effect of the Internet: bookstores are going out of business as well.

Unfortunately – or fortunately, I suppose, depending upon your viewpoint – we are spiraling into an all-electronic age. I have finally reached a point of acceptance with this. There is no stopping it at this point. Trying to stop it would be akin to standing in front of a fast-moving train.

I've seen what a train does to a penny laid upon the tracks. I'm not going to be the Penny trying to stand there.

Be that as it may, it is coming/already here.

Embrace it and become one with it. Life's just easier that way.

Self-Publishing: Wave of the Future

There is no greater agony than bearing an untold story inside you. ~Maya Angelou

My favorite argument for self-publishing is the money.

Before the Internet, publishers got 85% off the cost of each book sale. The author scored 15%.

Let's say your book costs $5.99. Your cut is approximately 89¢ per book sold.

Now let's say you have an agent who gets 20% of your take. That means that he or she gets 18¢ of each of the 89¢ you get. Your cut then becomes 71¢ per book.

Now that's not too bad. But let's consider what the publisher used to do for their 85%.

Back in the day, publishing houses were full service. Of course, they got copies of your book on bookshelves. Printing costs are exorbitant, so most of the 85% went to those costs.

However, publishers also had editors and graphic designers on staff to design the jacket and proofread and edit your work. Some of them probably still do, although from reading a few recently published books I find it questionable.

But publishers also did marketing, publicizing, and advertising. They set up book reviews and book signings. They promoted your book because they were also promoting themselves. They had other titles, maybe even some similar to your own, and if the reading public liked yours there were other books they could choose from to purchase.

Publishing houses still get 85% of each book sale. The difference now is that the majority of them expect the author to have a marketing and promotion plan, to set up his or her own book signings and book reviews: The author has to do the legwork publishers used to do.

This may seem fair to some, but if you're doing all that marketing and promoting, when do you have time to work on your next novel? Not to mention that many authors don't have the skills or background to accomplish these tasks (myself among them).

Self-publishing (also referred to as Print on Demand) is something of a double-edged sword: if you're going to be doing all the legwork yourself, why not do it all yourself? And give yourself a larger cut in the process. It still means you have to do all the legwork, but at least you get 100% of the profit. It also means you are solely responsible for preparing your book for publication whether it is for print or electronic distribution.

Here's how most of the self-publishers online work: there is a "base" price for each book depending upon number of pages and color included in the interior. When you publish the book, you mark up the sale price above this base price according to how much profit you wish to make.

I strongly caution everyone to not get carried away with this. Sure you can make a $10 profit on each sale provided you have written something that is very specialized, like car repair or something of that nature. But if you've written a murder mystery, don't allow greed to make you go crazy. Keep in mind the economy. Also keep in mind that if you make up to $2 per book sale, you're probably getting a better cut than a lot of authors receive through a publishing house.

With publishing houses going the way of the do-do bird, with the world headed towards everything electronic, self-publishing will one day be the way everyone gets published.

One really good thing about self-publishing: no more rejection letters or e-mails.

Anyone, and I do mean anyone, can self-publish. For better or for worse.

It is now a prerogative. It is no longer necessary to seek someone else's approval: approval which is based upon how much money they think your work will make them.

It is truly freedom of the press now.

So put it out there and see who salutes it!

Previewer Tools for Kindle Formatting for Amazon

Start writing, no matter what. The water does not flow until the faucet is turned on. ~Louis L'Amour

You are an author who wants to self-publish your book on Kindle and you have no idea where to start. This is for you.

Item No. 1

First on the agenda is to have Word on your computer. Unless you are a super-techno-geek who can compose an HTML document from the ground up, you will need Word because nothing else works with Kindle. Word 2010 (Home and Student version) and Word 2013 (Non-Commercial) both weigh in at less than $100. Shop around: you can often find them at discounted rates.

Item No. 2

Self-publishing for Kindle means you will need a way to get some idea of how your book will look for the Kindle platform. If you cannot afford a Kindle there are other ways to do this.

When your book is uploaded for Kindle on the Kindle Direct Publishing website (http://bit.ly/1qLEOM0) you have the option of previewing the book with the built-in Kindle previewer. However, the previewer has never worked when I have tried it.

Your other option is to download the Kindle Previewer (http://amzn.to/VRP214). You will need to scroll to the bottom of this page in order to download it. It is available for free.

I would suggest you also download Kindle for PC (http://amzn.to/18jXNqq). This allows you to view your book almost as an actual Kindle user might view it. I feel it gives a more accurate view of the finished product. However, keep in mind there is no guaranty it will actually look like that on a Kindle device. This, too, is downloadable for free.

Utilizing these two devices will be a huge help in determining how your book looks and what fixes you may need to make in order to get your book properly formatted.

Item No. 3

If you were not trained on how Word works, the process can be confusing. It's very easy to get lost, especially when it comes to placement of photographs, how to save the document and so on. I had my training on software which was much, much simpler than Word so deciphering the use of Word software was a real challenge for me.

It is twice as challenging when you are attempting to correctly format for Kindle.

There is yet another tool you can use which will simplify the process. *Building Your Book For Kindle* (http://amzn.to/VRPdJL) is available for free download. It has step by step instructions on how to set your paragraphs, how to create a table of contents, how to bookmark your table of contents, etc.

Online tutorials may be helpful, though most assume the student is somewhat familiar with Word.

If Word is a foreign language to you as it is to me, the best advice I can give to those not familiar with Word is to jump in there and play around with it. Figure out how it works. At least download the book and Kindle for PC. The instructions are simplified but not condescending. It will help to simplify the formatting process.

Formatting for Smashwords

Don't quit. It's very easy to quit during the first 10 years. Nobody cares whether you write or not, and it's very hard to write when nobody cares one way or the other. You can't get fired if you don't write, and most of the time you don't get rewarded if you do. But don't quit. ~Andre Dubus

We've covered some basic tools and formatting for Kindle publication for Amazon. Let's tackle formatting for Smashwords.

If you think formatting for Amazon is a trip, you ain't seen nothin' yet. Formatting for Smashwords is a whole different ball game.

There are a few tools that will help soften the process. It's best if you get these tools before you begin formatting.

But first, visit the Smashwords site. Meander a while. Download a few free books to get the look and feel of the formatting as well as find a few gems you might enjoy reading. Peruse the FAQ section and read some of the helpful articles listed there. You will find, much to your surprise and delight, that your digital book can be available to a number of electronic reading devices in addition to Kindle.

Get to know Smashwords. They are actually much more author- and reader-friendly than Amazon, they are quick to respond to queries and they have a great deal to offer, both authors and readers. But it is imperative that you make certain this is the route you wish to pursue. That decision is up to each individual and it is each individual's responsibility to be well-informed.

That said, first, download the *Smashwords Style Guide* by Smashwords founder Mark Coker (http://bit.ly/1cUB2tE). Read it before you begin formatting.

I must be honest here. I found reading the Guide a little difficult. Not because Mr. Coker didn't write it well but because I am a techno-clod and not a big fan of Word. I find navigating the program confusing at times. However, there are links within the Guide which direct you to visual instructions on YouTube. I actually found the visual instructions much more helpful and cannot tell you how much I appreciate the inclusion of those links.

Now that you have read the Guide, there are a couple of tools which might prove helpful during your formatting process.

Download Calibre (http://calibre-ebook.com/). This is a wonderful program which converts Word documents to MOBI and EPUB formats. It is free to download though they appreciate donations.

Next, you'll want to download Adobe Digital Reader (http://adobe.ly/1glOwxH). This is also free and will allow you to view your document in EPUB formats once it is converted.

Keep in mind when viewing your document(s) in your Kindle for PC and Adobe Digital Reader that 1) it may not necessarily make the grade, so to speak (more on that later) and 2) it still may not accurately reflect your document as it appears on other readers. However, it will help you find some of those trouble spots before you upload to Smashwords.

Great. You have your Style Guide, your Calibre, your Kindle for PC, and your Adobe Digital Reader. You're ready to get started.

When creating your document don't use tabs for paragraph indentations. This seems to be pretty much standard for all electronic devices. Don't use the ribbon across the top of your Word program to set up your document either. Set it up as follows:

On your Home tab, beneath the Heading 1, Heading 2 bar is the word Styles. To the right is a very small triangle with an arrow in it. Click on the arrow. This will bring up a list of choices. Beside each choice is an icon. Find the word NORMAL on that list. Place your cursor over the paragraph icon. It will change into an arrow. Click once on the arrow. This brings up a list of choices. Click on Modify in that list. A Modify Text box will pop up. In this box, select your font and font size. I use Times New Roman for everything. It's a time-old standard, professional and my personal choice. I also select 9pt for my font size. Remember, electronic devices are capable of enlarging or diminishing the size viewed on the screen. The font size 9pt reduces the size of your document even though you may have to enlarge it on your computer screen in order to view it yourself.

As I said, formatting for Smashwords is a completely different ball game. It is almost the complete opposite of formatting for Kindle for Amazon. Allow me to explain.

First, if you have Word 2010 you cannot upload this document to Smashwords. Word 2010 saves as a .docx document which Smashwords does not accept. Word 2003 is an acceptable format. Fortunately, 2010 allows you to save your document as a 2003 document. Once you do that, double check the formatting. Sometimes the text will reflow or formatting available in 2010 is not available for 2003 so it's always a good idea to look over your document before you attempt to convert.

If your Word program is prior to 2010, you don't have anything to worry about.

Once you've done this, use Calibre to convert your document. It comes with instructions on how to do this. It's actually pretty easy once you get the hang of it. Once they're converted you can then check them in your Kindle for PC and Adobe Digital Reader.

Check each and every page of your document in both readers. Ensure all text is consistent, i.e., same point size, same font (with the possible exception of headlines), look for blank pages that shouldn't be blank, and make certain your images, if any, are in line with text. (I learned this the hard way, more on that later).

If you spot anything, go back and fix it, convert it and check it again. This will save you a lot of aggravation and headache when you upload those documents to Smashwords.

A couple of tips before you convert.

1: Your Table of Contents, if you have one, MUST be manually bookmarked and hyperlinked. It's not so bad really, unless you have 64 chapters to bookmark and hyperlink. It can be very tedious. Luckily, I have a music playlist titled "Music to Word By" that I use specifically for times like this.

2. Your images MUST be formatted "In Line With Text." If they are not, your document will be rejected until you've fixed it.

Okay, you've done all the conversions, checked everything and it all looks good. You're ready to upload.

Remember this word: **AutoVetter**.

This is the "more on that later" part.

This is the program used at Smashwords to initially determine if your book is acceptable. It is also the program which will tell you what, if anything, is wrong with your document. It will tell you what the problem is and what needs to be fixed. You will then be tasked with going back, resolving the issue or issues and re-uploading your document.

If your images are not In Line With Text, your document will be rejected until you have them all In Line With Text. Also, make sure your images are .JPEGS. The Guide states that .PNG works best. However, I received an e-mail telling me that .JPEGS work best. So use .JPEGS.

You may end up having to re-upload your document a number of times. Or you may not if you have understood the requirements and followed them.

That was my problem. It isn't that I'm an idiot and can't follow instructions. The instructions elude me at times and Word consternates me.

But I'm getting over that. I have learned more about Word than I ever really cared to know. My program of choice, QuarkXPress, is on a dinosaur of a computer on its last legs. I shudder at the thought of one day booting up that computer and it simply will not. Therefore, it is imperative that I learn how to use Word, like it or not.

Necessity is such a mother.

Be that as it may, making work available on Smashwords offers an author so many avenues that it is truly one of the wisest choices an independent author can make. Competition being as fierce as it is, the independent author must explore every avenue available to her or him if she or he wishes to be successful.

Smashwords offers a wide variety of distribution. As every author knows, the more exposure, the better chance for success. And Smashwords doesn't demand exclusivity.

Why Limit Yourself?

Closed in a room, my imagination becomes the universe, and the rest of the world is missing out. ~Criss Jami

For years, I had my digital books enrolled in KDP Select. Why? For the simple reason that when I began self-publishing in 2010 – a mere four years ago – Smashwords was still in the process of growing pains. I didn't even hear about Smashwords until a couple of years ago.

My hesitancy to get on board with Smashwords was all about my lack of confidence in my technical abilities. I'm still not confident that I'm capable of doing this right, I'm just more daring these days (surviving a heart attack sometimes has that effect on people).

Be that as it may, I'm willing to try almost anything to get my work out there, noticed and purchased and/or appreciated.

Oh, hold on a second. There's a little caveat here. According to KDP Select, an author is not allowed to have her work available for any other electronic platform or retailer except KDP Select through Amazon. If she does and Amazon finds out, she will no longer be allowed to publish through Amazon.

There wasn't even a question of what to do. I opted out of KDP Select and waited for the current contracts on each book to expire. They automatically renew every 90 days so I didn't have long to wait.

I wanted more choices, more opportunities to make my work available, more exposure. In short, a better chance that people will read, enjoy and appreciate my work.

Amazon doesn't offer that. They publish exclusively for Kindle devices because Kindle is a product of Amazon. Naturally, they want their readers to purchase electronic books from them.

And this, my friends, drastically limits an author's visibility.

And that isn't fair to the independent author.

I remember back in the day when Amazon was just a baby with not many titles from which to choose. Those titles were only from major traditional publishing houses. Yes, it was a long time ago in a galaxy far, far away.

I have the experience of having watched throughout the years as Amazon expanded and became this humongous corporate entity. They may put Walmart out of business one day. A frightening thought, at least to me.

I am not bashing Amazon. I like Amazon.

I like Smashwords as well. I like what Smashwords has to offer. Distribution on a variety of platforms, including libraries; availability of books for free, the list goes on.

This takes a great deal of legwork off the author. I cannot tell you how many hours I have spent researching ways to get word of my books to other outlets, including libraries. The research never paid off. It is virtually impossible for an independent author to get her work on library shelves or available to other electronic platforms on her own. The best I could do was to get my books on the "Local Author Shelf" at my local library.

There is one disadvantage to Smashwords that I hope may change in the future. They pay authors for their sales on a quarterly basis. More precisely, within 30-40 days after the end of each quarter. It isn't such a bad thing, really. It allows time for sales to accumulate so the earnings are bigger. But it is nice when Amazon deposits your sales into your account at the end of the month following the sales. Even if it is only a few bucks or so. Every little bit helps.

The important thing is to not paint yourself into a corner. Exclusivity is a limited option which doesn't guarantee an independent author the exposure she or he needs. Multiple exposure doesn't guarantee sales but it will improve your chances of getting your work noticed.

And every independent author deserves that chance.

Creating a Complete Book Cover in Word

Disclaimer: I created a full book cover – front, spine and back – in Word 2010. I have no other versions of Word so I have no way of knowing how this would work in earlier versions.

Creating a book cover in Word can be a daunting task, especially when you are accustomed to using programs much easier than Word. But it is possible. Not easy. But possible.

The first thing you need to do is figure out the size of your book. Is it standard paperback size – 5x7? Or are you going with a 6x9 format? Number of pages?

Because the first thing you need to do is figure out the size of the Word document you will use to create your book cover: The complete size including the spine and back page.

Visit www.createspace.com. Under the Books tab click on Publish a Trade Paperback. In the line of tabs across the center of the page click on Cover. Under this section click on submission requirements. This will give you step by step instructions on how to calculate the spine width of your book. It is based upon the total number of pages and type of paper you choose. You don't have to be logged in or even a member to take advantage of this tool.

As a general rule, the spine width will be about 1" – 1 1/2" depending upon the size of your book. Books with less than 75 pages do not require a spine. If you're uploading to Create Space, you'll want to be as exact as possible. Otherwise, you'll receive an email from the Create Space team telling you to fix the spine.

Going forward, my document size was a total of 15.9x6. My spine width was 1.5".

There is a step by step video on YouTube which is very good for creating the front cover of a book. However, if you have no other option than to create the full cover yourself, which is necessary if you are creating a print book, you'll need to create the entire thing.

The YouTube video: How To Make Your Own Book Covers In MS Word by Mandee Kulp is an excellent tutorial: (http://bit.ly/VVoNHe) to help get you started. However, the tutorial is for the front cover only.

Before you begin placing the elements on your front and back pages, do the spine first.

Draw a text box the height of your book and the width of your spine.

Type the title of your book and your name.

1. When you draw the text box, the Drawing Tools tab appears at the top of the ribbon. There is a text direction tab to the left of the Position tab. Click on the Text Direction tab and choose Rotate All Text 90 degrees. This will position the text within the spine area sideways.

2. Now make your text the size and font you want it. Place spaces between the title and your name. Center the text, but keep in mind it will not be centered within the overall scope of your book. You will need to center that text yourself. Calculate the exact center of your document according to its width. When you place the spine, click on the ruler above it at the center point. This will show a tab ruler going down the document. If the text of your spine is in the center of this ruler, you've got it. If it isn't keep shifting it until it does appear in the center.

3. Don't forget to click on Shape Outline and select No Outline to remove the border around the text box. Also use the Shape Fill tool if you want your spine to have a color; choose No Outline if you wish for it to be white. If

you want the spine in a different color simply choose that color.

Now place your images and text on the front and back pages. Some weird things may happen when you do this. Your spine may shift from its location; text boxes may disappear. The best I can tell you is to experiment with the Wrap Text and Position tabs until everything stays in its place. You may need to choose In Front of Text or Behind Text. When you go under the Wrap Text icon, the list gives you the choice of More Layout Options at the bottom. You may have to remove the Distance from Text, putting a zero value in all boxes in order to stop the shifting of other elements. This may force you to hard return some text but it is the only way I could find to make it work so the spine wouldn't shift.

Once you have completed your book cover save it as a Word document, then save it as a PDF. When you save a Word document as a PDF, you will need to embed the fonts. This is how you do that:

Click on File > Save As > and choose .PDF as the file type
Check the Optimize for Standard option
Click the drop down arrow for Tools (next to the Save button) and select Save Options
Check Embed all fonts in this file
Uncheck Do not embed common system fonts'
Click OK
Click the Save button

You are now ready to upload your completed PDF book cover.

But what if you need a .JPEG image? You'll need one to upload the front for display.

But Acrobat Reader doesn't allow you to save a PDF as a .JPEG. Word has no method of saving documents as images either.

Believe it or not, that is actually fairly simple to accomplish.

You will want to create a "print screen" of your document. Be sure your entire document appears on the screen. The key to do a print screen is usually located to the right of the F12 key along the top of your keyboard. It is most often labeled "prt scrn." Press that key.

When you press that key nothing will appear to have happened. But your computer has saved the screen image to the Clipboard.

Now open the Paint program, usually located under "Accessories" on your Startup menu. The Paint program is part of the Microsoft Windows package and should be on your computer if you're using Microsoft.

When you have Paint open, hold down the Control key and press the letter V. This will paste the screen print into the Paint program.

Now crop the image so that only your book cover appears. Now you can Save as .JPEG, .PNG. .GIF or .BMP. You can further crop the image so that only the front cover is visible and save it in those formats as well. Just remember to give the file a different name so you don't overwrite the full cover.

Yes, I freely admit it isn't the greatest cover. As a matter of fact, it's terrible. But it was something I threw together to see if it could be done. With more practice and better images, I can do better.

And so can you.

The Muse

He asked, "What makes a man a writer?" I said, "it's simple.
You either get it down on paper, or jump off a bridge."
~Charles Bukowski

The Muse Speaks

Your intuition knows what to write, so get out of the way.
~Ray Bradbury

The word muse can be used as either verb or noun.

As a verb, it means "to think or meditate in silence, as on some subject."

As a noun: "the goddess or the power regarded as inspiring a poet, artist, thinker, or the like."

Both definitions apply to writers and other people of creative thought processes. Creative people must spend a good deal of time thinking about the next step in her or his creative process.

We also call upon our individual creative goddesses from time to time.

My creative muse's name is Natalie (that's what she told me). She is one of the most important people I know.

She virtually shouts at me when a new idea is presented to me as a possible creative avenue to pursue. But she also, very quietly, works on ideas teaming up with my subconscious to ensure those ideas are coherent and worthy when it comes time for me to consciously work on them.

They make a great team, Natalie and my subconscious. Often is the time that an idea will occur to me during my writing that I had not consciously considered. I credit Nat and Sub for holding on to that idea to present to me just when I needed it.

It is important to listen to the muse. She is very wise and knows what the creative person needs. She probably knows you better than you know yourself.

She will inspire you, sometimes taking you in directions you wouldn't normally venture to follow.

She'll never steer you wrong. But she'll always steer you in the right direction.

At times, a writer gets "married" to a particular idea. A character must act a certain way or these particular events must happen thusly. Though still being creative, this line of thinking leaves little room for digression, expansion or exploration: it limits the imagination and demands that certain steps be taken without allowing new steps to be created.

Follow where the muse takes you. She may be trying to show you a different perspective, one which might make all the difference. She may be introducing you to a new character, one which you didn't think of but one which might add more to the story than you realize.

She may be encouraging you to experiment. Try something different, something new. She may be prompting you to use a storyline that others think nominal but which you can make astounding.

Granted, these days the muse may communicate with you via Smartphone, iPad or even a posting on Facebook. Sometimes I think it's more difficult to hear the muse with all the electronic traffic scampering across the surface. But you learn to listen for the muse. You recognize her voice and you can hear it above all the electronic signals. You'll hear her in a news report; in a snippet of conversation. You may recognize her in a Facebook posting or an item of interest delivered to your Smartphone.

Regardless of how your muse communicates, the muse has faith in you even when you lack faith in yourself. She knows what you can do, what you are capable of, even though you may be unaware of your capabilities.

She is there to believe in you when no one else does.

So when the muse speaks: Listen.

So, You Want to be a Writer?

We don't create a fantasy world to escape reality, we create it to be able to stay. ~Lynda Barry

Welcome to Euphoria.
Welcome to Hades.
It is definitely both.
It takes a person of strength and character to dedicate herself or himself to writing.

It is totally, completely, absolutely euphoric to write. Writing the tragedies of others helps you forget your own. You experience adventure by writing your characters' adventures. You can safely express your feelings by projecting them onto a fictitious character.

Be forewarned. Writing that novel requires hours of solitude. It is not a bad thing, but if you don't like spending a lot of time alone it may be difficult for you.

It also means sacrifice. You may have to turn off that television set or monitor your time on the Internet in order to get something accomplished.

It doesn't mean you can't spend time with friends and family. But it may mean you'll have to miss out on a thing or two once in a while.

It may mean losing sleep. Maybe not by your own choice. Sometimes the characters or events in your novel are enough to keep you awake and writing in your head. The plot or a particular situation keeps going around and around in your mind until you simply cannot tolerate it any longer and must get up to write it down because if you don't you may forget half of what you want to write. You'll nod off at work the next day but at least you get it out of your system.

There will be times when you don't feel like writing. You don't even want to boot up your computer or even pick up a pen to jot something down. You may feel you need to take a break, take a walk or take a shot of Jack Daniels. Or maybe even all three at the same time.

Now the book is complete. Hades begins.

Now comes the marketing and promoting of your book. The attempt to generate interest and book sales.

For some, this may be the most difficult part.

No one is going to "stumble" upon your book and think it is wonderful. It isn't going to take off overnight. There is a great deal of work ahead.

Sometimes getting family and friends to read your book is a challenge. Everyone is busy and few have the time required to actually read a novel. If you can get them to do it and write a review, consider yourself lucky.

Get involved in every social media site you can stomach. Facebook, Twitter, Google+, Pinterest. Start a blog about writing or a personal blog. Wordpress is my favorite. Join Goodreads and do a giveaway of your book. Submit your writing to StumbleUpon and Digg.

Be forewarned. Joining those social media sites and blogging is very time-consuming. It is a monster that will take a big chunk out of the time you set aside for writing. That isn't to say it isn't enjoyable or fruitful. But it is majorly time-consuming.

There are also book signings, book readings and other events to plan and attend.

It can be very aggravating and discouraging, especially when you see little or no results for your attempts.

But, let me assure you, when you hold your published book in your hands, everything, and I do mean *everything*, you have experienced and endured, will experience and will endure, is worth it.

It is your legacy. A little piece of yourself that will stand for all time.

I'm sure when Sir Arthur Conan Doyle wrote his Sherlock Holmes stories or "Lost World" he wasn't aware they would someday be considered classics. The same for Edgar Allen Poe or Mark Twain or Jules Verne or any number of writers.

Who knows? In a hundred years or so, your book may be considered a classic.

Why would anyone put herself or himself through all like this? Because if writers didn't write we would explode. It's that simple.

So you want to be a writer? It is a trip between Euphoria and Hades on an almost daily basis. But the scenery along the way can be life-affirming, life-altering and just plain interesting.

Go for it!

Before You Start Writing

There is nothing to writing. All you do is sit down at a typewriter and bleed. ~Ernest Hemingway

Before you have written your first words on paper, allow me to give you a few tips that will save you a lot of aggravation in the long run.

Get a Website

Whether you do it yourself or get someone else to do it for you, get a website. It doesn't matter that you haven't written anything yet, get one anyway. Especially if you know you're going to do a lot of writing. You can post a daily blog on it or photos or something until you get the books finished. Once you have completed your books and they are ready it will be much simpler to upload information about them if you already have a website. Just make sure your website has an attractive professional look to it. You can always update or expand it once your books start selling.

Get some Business Cards

Vistaprint has many interesting designs these days at relatively inexpensive rates. I checked out Vistaprint when it was new and nothing was there specifically for writers. Now there are several very nice designs that will show you are a writer. Some can be customized with a quote (for free) and upgraded to look very professional and unique. You can design the business cards yourself and have them printed elsewhere. Whichever choice you make, those business cards are a necessity. Hand them out to everyone you meet.

Build a Network

Whether it is via social media or live in-person networking, do it. Interact with these people often, if not daily via social websites. Those business cards will be great handouts at personal networking events. Facebook, Google+, Twitter, Pinterest just to name a few allow you to share photos, comments, likes, stories or whatever suits you. The importance of this is that once you have finished that book and gotten it out there, these are the people who will show you support and, hopefully, help get the word out about your work. The following you build prior to publishing your book will be more supportive than those who follow you after the book is published.

Regardless of what anyone tells you, it is time-consuming and oftentimes drudgery but it will help you in the future.

Self-Publishing

Regardless of what anyone else says, self-publishing is the wave of the future. Traditional publishing houses are going the way of the do-do bird. These establishments will one day be extinct. It may yet take some time, but it is coming. Create Space is a subsidiary of Amazon and the publishing format I use. Automatically, your book is available on Amazon, the largest retailer on the Internet. This, too, is something of note: Amazon may someday be the *only* retailer on the Internet.

Self-publishing allows you to set the price of your book thereby determining the profit you wish to make. Keep it modest. A $10 profit on each book sale is greed, pure and simple, and guarantees you will have no sales at all.

Plan an event

Look ahead to the time when you have that book completed and published. How are you going to get the word out? Bring attention to yourself and your work? Can you tie your book in with current events or other media?

This is something you should consider prior to writing your book or, at the very least, while you're writing your book.

It has been stated numerous times that word of mouth is the best way to create that much-needed author exposure. While I don't completely agree with that I don't completely disagree with it, either. It is as difficult to get word of mouth recommendations as it is any other marketing.

Plan an event around your book. A book reading, a book signing, a class at a local school, be part of a literary festival, send press releases to local media, schedule a talk on a local radio/tv show to discuss your book. Heck, have a yard sale and give away a few copies of your book along with your business card or any other materials related to your book.

Then plan another event. The more events you have or attend, the more exposure you will get for your writing.

Why Do This Before You Start Writing?

I am one of those people who did none of this prior to publishing any of my books. I began self-publishing in 2009 and simply had no idea to do any of this. Playing "catch-up" is much too overwhelming. I am buried in the attempt to understand and use the social media. I get very little results but I am certain that is due to my lack of being accustomed to it. Time restraints don't allow me to spend as much energy on the social media sites as is purportedly required.

Get an early start on it and get used to it. Your path to being a successful writer will be much smoother.

The Muse at Work

*At night, when the objective world has slunk back into its
cavern and left dreamers to their own, there come inspirations
and capabilities impossible at any less magical and quiet hour.
No one knows whether or not he is a writer unless he has tried
writing at night. ~H.P. Lovecraft*

The characters in *Nero's Fiddle* are issued the challenge to
get to Washington, DC within 25-30 days to stop a disastrous
incident. They must walk almost the entire 600 miles. The novel
rounds out at 180,000 words.

I encountered a dilemma during the writing. I wanted a
particular reaction from the lead character, Captain Beverly
Mossberg, USMC. However, the reaction I wanted would leave
her children thinking her a coward.

The scenario: Bev encounters no fewer than a dozen men
molesting a young woman. All men are carrying guns. Bev has
her own gun and is an expert markswoman but the odds are not in
her favor. As with most women (including myself), her initial gut
reaction is to charge into the fray, gun blazing. Doing that
however would risk the lives of her children as well as risk
making them orphans. There's no help in sight: Sedona (a
tagalong stranger who later becomes part of the family) is akin to
Don Knotts in *The Shakiest Gun in the West* and there's no way to
call for help.

Initially, I wanted Bev to reluctantly walk away, feeling it
was the only way to protect her children. The more I considered
that option the more I realized how unsatisfying it was. It would
create a great deal of conflict between Bev and her kids,
especially her twelve year old daughter, which would make for
great drama, but it didn't present Bev as the kick-ass solider I
knew her to be.

I asked a few women their opinion of the situation and what they would do. Most of them found it as problematic as I did. Their initial gut reaction was to start a gunfight but, with kids in tow, they'd be afraid to. All of them were opposed to the idea of walking away but none of them would put their children's lives at risk by attacking the men first. All of them felt, as I did, there had to be a viable solution.

I did what I always do when faced with such an enigmatic dilemma: I sat on it for a few days and asked my muse to work on it for me.

My muse came through. Yes, Bev initially is going to walk away. But one of the men stumbles upon her and the others when he walks into the woods to relieve himself. When the man threatens her daughter, Cap'n Mossy is forced to react. Her actions not only enable the girl to get away, she also takes care of the threatening men. In addition, the solution presented to me by my muse allowed me to satisfy my desire to have Bev blow something up. (Make no mistake, Bev wanted to blow something up, too).

And that's all I'm going to reveal about that.

It pays to ask the muse for help: to stand down from the writing even if for only a short period of time. It's that subconscious thing at work again: that part of the brain that works non-stop on whatever dilemmas we're facing and sometimes offers us solutions to difficult situations.

I just need to train it to work that way in real life.

Subconscious Working Overtime?
It's Supposed To!

Creativity involves breaking out of established patterns in order to look at things in a different way. ~Edward de Bono

The subconscious mind is a marvelous thing. According to crime dramas, the subconscious mind is capable of remembering everything we see, hear and learn in our lifetime. We may not be able to consciously recall the tag number of that car that cut us off in traffic, but our subconscious never forgets.

I rely a great deal on my subconscious to enhance my writing. It never fails when I am at a crossroads with my characters, a solution seems to magically be made known to me. Accordingly, I credit my subconscious.

This was really brought home to me when I recently revised a couple of novels published prior to the *Sword of Tilk Trilogy.*

I reread *9.5B* first published in 2010. I created a character named Stormy Rose Prometheus. Excuse me, *Dr.* Stormy Rose Prometheus who was known by the moniker Prometheus.

I didn't do any research on the name when I initially wrote the book. I don't know why. I am usually anal about that sort of thing, but I liked the name.

Before I began revising the book, I took to the Internet to find out exactly who and what Prometheus was. I especially wanted to know because there was a movie released in 2012 of the same name and I needed to know if any part of the movie overlapped the book and vice versa. What I found surprised me.

Prometheus was a Titan from Greek mythology credited with the creation of man. He gave the gift of fire to mankind then was punished by the Greek gods for doing so. He was tied to a rock and an eagle would eat his liver. The liver then grew back and the eagle returned each day to feast upon the organ again.

I remember studying Greek mythology in high school. I recall being in a cramped little room, sweltering from the heat even with the windows open, desks crowded side by side against one another. I even remember the cover of the book: kind of a peach and teal color, very pretty I thought. But I do not for the life of me *consciously* recall the name Prometheus.

But we must have studied Prometheus at some point. The name obviously stuck.

I also learned from my research that the original title of Mary Shelley's *Frankenstein* was *Frankenstein: The Modern Prometheus*. The subtitle has been dropped but it refers to Victor Frankenstein himself due to his attempt to create life through scientific means or by means other than natural reproduction. It is a similar credit given to Prometheus the Titan when he created man from clay: a being into which a spirit could be breathed.

The irony of naming my character Prometheus surprised me. You see, Dr. Stormy Rose Prometheus is also a scientist. One who clones herself a daughter.

There are many other smaller examples of my subconscious contributing to my writing efforts, some of which came directly from personal experience. But the Prometheus name really took me by surprise.

I have learned to sort of "listen" to my subconscious when I'm writing. If I am struggling with a scene, a dialogue or a character, I sit very still. I allow my imagination to visualize the idea I am attempting to get on paper.

Before I know it, I am breezing through the scenario with ideas that had not occurred to me but which work very well with what I am writing.

Some call it inspiration. Some call it a muse. It's really both.

No matter what you choose to call it, pay attention when it comes calling. More than likely, it's your subconscious working overtime.

That's what it's there for.

Get More Writing Time Out of Your Day

Writing is a socially acceptable form of schizophrenia.
~E.L. Doctorow

Everybody's busy. Between working, going to school, taking kids to baseball practice, ballet, the library, grocery shopping, doing laundry and a myriad of sundry chores, who has time to write?

Answer: You do.

I, too, often find myself pressed for time. There are ways of squeezing in extra time for writing.

1. Pens and paper.

Most writers know to keep pens and a small notebook handy to jot down the occasional idea, but not many realize how valuable these tools are. Invented long before the computer age, these two items are much easier to carry around than even a laptop, are much more lightweight, do not require electricity or a signal and the batteries never die. The pen may occasionally run out of ink, but that's why you always carry extras. I suggest using a steno pad or one of those small fat notebooks that fit easily into a purse, tote bag, briefcase or even your pocket.

Though it may seem outdated or archaic to some to use pens and paper, they are still more convenient to use than a laptop while commuting or on your lunch break. It is also guaranteed that few would attempt to steal a notebook and pen right out of your hands as they might a laptop or other electronic device.

2. Commuting

Speaking of commuting, if you have access to public transportation, consider using it. Take those pens and pads with you. You will be amazed at how much writing you can accomplish if you leave the driving to someone else.

Within one week, I filled half a steno pad with writing. I can write very small and cramped when I need to in order to make the most use of a notebook. The pages I had written equated to 50 typewritten 8.5 x 11 pages. Those 50 typewritten pages were then equivalent to 80 pages in a 5 x 8 inch format. It brought the total page count of my novel very close to 300 pages. That was just in one week of writing during my commute and lunch breaks.

3. Get up early or stay up late.

Buy yourself a half hour of writing time by setting the alarm clock half an hour earlier. If you have kids or other people to care for, make sure it's half an hour before everyone else gets up. Or stay up half an hour after everyone else has gone to bed. This may be a good time to do some research for some of those writing projects. Either way, focus on your writing project for that half hour and you'll get a lot more done than you think.

4. Fifteen minutes.

Force yourself to take those two fifteen (or ten) minute breaks at your job. It may not seem like very long, but you can get a good bit of writing done when you focus on it for ten or fifteen minutes. If nothing else, it will allow you time to focus on an idea or a character long enough to get some thoughts organized for later writing. Those fifteen minutes of writing could very well lead to your fifteen minutes of fame someday.

5. Waiting Time.

Waiting to see the doctor, dentist or any other appointment, waiting for a train or a bus, waiting on hold: all these are excellent opportunities to get some writing done. Everyone knows that, even when you show up early for an appointment, chances are you are going to be waiting for at least a good fifteen or twenty minutes or even longer. Use that time to work on your writing project. Whether it is three minutes or thirty minutes, use it to your advantage.

What can I write in three minutes, you may ask? I wrote a complete dialogue between two people by writing one or two lines during the 45 seconds it took the MARTA train to pull into the Five Points station; each day for a week I wrote one or two lines during that 45 seconds. Yes, it needed a little work afterwards, but I got the basics down. It can be done.

6. Lunch breaks.

A half hour or an hour lunch break can be an excellent time to move your writing project along. If you like taking lunch with your co-workers, it's an excellent break, but take at least one or two lunch breaks during the week to spend some time working on your writing.

7. Weekends and Holidays.

A prime time for those of us working during the week to catch up on some writing. Let it be known that you will be spending some time during the weekend, even if it is only a few hours, to write. Hire a babysitter for the kids or arrange for them to have a play date with some friends. Send the spouse out shopping. Ask for the cooperation you need to do what you need to do. Chances are, if you've been writing during the week, you will have a good bit of writing that needs to be typed, organized, fleshed out or completed.

No, don't spend the entire weekend or holiday writing. After all, everybody needs a little downtime. But at least consider setting aside a certain number of uninterrupted hours for your writing. You'll be glad you did when everything begins to come together.

8. Using Notepad on your Computer.

If your job requires you to spend a lot of time on the computer, keep the Notepad program open. Notepad is a word processing program found on PCs. I believe Macs come with Wordpad. Either way, keep that program open. If you are like many writers, your writing projects are always on your mind; kind of like one of those programs on a computer which run in the background. The Notepad on your computer is similar to a pad and pen: it comes in handy to jot down quick ideas or snippets of dialogue, things that will only take a quick moment to make a note of. This is NOT to suggest you attempt to write an entire novel while you're at work. You need that job to pay the bills until you become a best-selling author. This is merely to make those quick notes of things you don't want to forget.

At the end of the day, copy and paste all your notes into an email and send it to yourself at your personal email address. If your company does not allow you to email yourself, print out your notes and take them home where you can organize and work on them.

I have created an entire list of potential character names by doing this. Ironically, the names are actually typos I have come across or done myself in my data entry job.

Though it may seem as though you are working all the time, you'll still have plenty of "downtime" on days when you don't feel like writing or aren't inspired to write. But on those days when you do feel like writing, you can steal time even if it is only ten minutes here or fifteen minutes there.

Stealing those precious minutes is an investment in yourself as a writer. By stealing those minutes, you'll be amazed at how much writing you can accomplish. Like pennies, those minutes do add up.

Writing Prompts

Great work doesn't make me jealous; it makes me want to work.
~Glen Hirshberg

I have had many people tell me, "*I want to be a writer.*" This is, more times than not, followed by, "*But I have no idea what to write about.*"

My initial gut reaction would be to say, "*You have GOT to be kidding!*" Because there are not enough hours in the day for me to write all that I wish to write about.

I exercise restraint when confronted with this situation. I don't want to discourage anyone from writing. But a died-in-the-wool writer would never make such a statement.

I do realize there are times when writers encounter lulls in their writing: times when the mind goes completely blank and the writer doesn't know where to begin.

Here are a few ideas for writing exercises that my kick-start your creative muse and get you out of that lull:

A childhood memory
Favorite recipes
Places you have visited
Places you would like to visit
A teacher who influenced you
A sad experience
A beloved pet
A best friend
A favorite book or movie
A high school crush
Setting a goal
Reaching a goal
Write a story about what is in a photograph
Give models in ads names, characteristics and backgrounds

Do the same for a stranger you see while out and about

This is only a handful of ideas to use for writing practice so you can get to working on that big writing project. The Internet is littered with writing prompt ideas.

If that's not enough, research the news for topics, trends, celebrity gossip and other items of interest.

And if all else fails, there's always the weather.

Use whatever it takes to get the creative juices flowing.

The Creation of Characters

On characters: You do everything you can to raise them right, and as soon as they hit the page they do any damn thing they please. ~Unknown

Establishing a Character's Character

*Tomorrow may be hell, but today was a good writing day, and on
the good writing days nothing else matters. ~Neil Gaiman*

Characters must have character.

This may seem an obvious statement, but you'd be surprised
how many writers fail to give their characters character.

You must ask yourself what characteristics do I want my
characters to have? The answer to that is completely up to you.

Determine if your character is a good guy/girl or a bad
guy/girl.

A good character may have some of the following
characteristics: Integrity, Courage, Loyalty, Determination,
Ambition, Compassion.

A bad character may have some of these: Greed, Hate, Anger,
Deceit, Ruthlessness, Dishonesty.

Mind you, characters will more than likely not be this cookie-
cutter. And these are just a few of the traits found in each
category. But if you're trying to establish who the reader should
root for, then each of your characters needs some of these traits.

Let's begin with the good guy.

The last thing you want to do is state, "She or he was loyal,
brave and true." She or he may be all three but it's a very boring
way to let the reader know.

Instead, put the character into a situation that shows the
reader how loyal, brave and true she or he is. Like in the
paragraph below.

*Donovan crept along the cobblestone path to the door of the
castle, his hand ever ready on the hilt of his sword. Dawn was
fast approaching. He had to get inside, kill the wizard Morgrith
and flee before the wizard's demons found him. He knew he could
do this. He must do this. Otherwise, Morgrith would cast a spell
rendering King Rodolfo powerless, incapable of running the*

kingdom. Even so, Donovan's hand trembled upon the hilt. He knew not what he would encounter in the castle, only that he would deal with whatever lay before him.

We have established that our hero, Donovan, is afraid; his hand would not tremble upon the hilt of his sword if he weren't afraid. His courage is evident in that he is willing to act in the face of his fear regardless of what he may encounter. His loyalty is to King Rodolfo and he will see his mission through.

Let's tackle the flip side of the coin. It isn't enough to state that someone is evil. Show the evil.

Morgrith stood at the window of his study following Donovan's every move. The demons stood at the ready, awaiting Morgrith's signal to begin their assault. There was a vat of hot boiling oil and talons and teeth sharpened to a fine point awaiting the beleaguered hero. Let him think one lowly knight could thwart this wizard's plans to possess the kingdom. He would know otherwise soon enough.

Here we've established the evil in our wizard. He's ready to kill one knight and it shows he will stop at nothing to get what he wants.

In order to develop a character's character, it is vital to force the character into challenging situations. How the character deals with those situations will establish the character of the character, for better or for worse.

It gives the reader a glimpse into the life of the character, what makes the character who she or he is. It enhances the reading experience to know a character will face her or his demons and will be a stronger person for having defeated those demons. It enhances the reading experience even more to see how a character deals with her or his demons.

Because how a character in a story or a novel deals with those challenging situations may well inspire a reader with new ideas about how to deal with her or his own challenging situations.

Giving Your Characters Blemishes

Which of us has not felt that the character we are reading in the printed page is more real than the person standing beside us?
~Cornelia Funke

This doesn't mean covering your character's face with adulthood acne or rosacea. But it doesn't mean all of your characters should have clear skin and picture-perfect white smiles either.

Giving a character a distinctive trait or traits, whether physical, mental or emotional, makes them more relatable for the reader.

Consider this character:

Daphne stood tall and erect, her slender body succinctly outlined by her flowing blue dress. She waited beneath the awning to avoid the rain. She sighed. Once again, she had forgotten her umbrella.

No matter, really. Sooner or later, some man or other, whether handsome or not, would come along and offer her his umbrella. Her smooth face and sapphire blue eyes guaranteed it.

And she would accept the offer, of course, knowing it gave the impression to the male that she was interested. When nothing could be further from the truth.

Consider this character:

Though short in stature, Colt was built solid: concrete wall solid. His tattered grimy flannel shirt stretched tautly across his chest. Faded denim jeans bulged from muscular legs, even though the jeans appeared to have been used for car waxing and worn afterwards without a good washing. His sandy brown hair was long and askew about his face. He wasn't old but his face gave the impression he was old beyond his years. His hazel eyes suggested a tired wisdom he would sooner live without. A raspy sound issued from his hand brushing across the salt and pepper beard on his face. He was a handsome man, though none could tell past the grime. A shower, shave and a haircut would not improve his outlook but it would well improve the way others looked at him.

Even so, none of these features compared with the constant twitch of his right eye. One would think he was winking in a suggestive manner if one didn't know any better.

What can you tell right away from the description of these characters?

Daphne may appear picture-perfect, but right away you know that Daphne is shallow and superficial. She's confident her good looks will get her the things she needs as well as the things she wants. She obviously doesn't hesitate to use them, particularly in regards to the opposite sex.

Daphne's good looks become her blemishes. Sooner or later she is bound to learn that good looks don't get her everything.

Colt, on the other hand, is fraught with obvious blemishes, from his slovenly appearance to his twitching eye. You get the impression that Colt has a story. His character is all the more interesting for his blemishes: why is he so slovenly when he obviously takes care of his body? He must take care of his body if he is so muscular. And why does his eye constantly twitch? What causes that?

Wonderful examples of imperfect (by society's definition) characters can be found in the works of Dean Koontz.

In By the Light of the Moon, the character Shep O'Connor suffers from Asperger Syndrome. In One Door Away From Heaven, Mickey Bellsong is a recovering alcoholic who meets up with Leilani, a little girl with a brace on her leg and a deformed hand.

These three characters are instrumental to their respective stories.

Shep provides a little comic relief when he is a walking thesaurus. But he also paints the picture of frustration for his older brother Dylan who is his caregiver. When the two undergo serious psychological changes after being given a shot of a mysterious fluid by a stranger, the relationship between the brothers is taken to an entirely new level as is Shep's character.

The relationship between Mickey and Leilani is fraught with humor when the two meet. But it is humor which hides each of the characters' worst fears. Leilani fears her stepfather is going to kill her. Mickey fears herself more than anything else. Little do these two characters know, the humor also hides their courage and strengths as well.

The shortcomings of all these characters is evident from minute one. It is a wonderful place to start as the reader experiences the growth of these characters and inevitably grows with them.

Picture-perfect characters are all fine and good. But characters with flaws are the characters readers will best relate to. An imperfect character makes for a stronger reader-character relationship.

Those flaws in the hero or protagonist make him or her human. It helps the reader realize that he or she can be the hero, too.

Give Readers an Idea of Your Character's Looks

Description begins in the writer's imagination, but should finish in the reader's. ~Stephen King

More and more often, I read books where description of a character is nonexistent. Is this a trend? Has someone changed the rules and I didn't get the memo?

It isn't necessary to go into vivid detailed description of how a character looks. But the essentials would be helpful to the reader.

At the very least, include the bare essentials: Height, weight, hair color, eye color, and ethnicity give the reader an idea of how a character looks.

No, looks are not everything. But I like to get a mental picture while reading a book. Having no description to go by is almost like trying to visualize a ghost.

Think of it this way. When a reader picks up your book, it's a lot like going on a blind date. The reader has no idea what she or he is getting into. If you want this blind date to go well you'll have to give the reader a lot more than she or he bargained for. Giving a description of your character is a good place to start.

Imagine, if you will, you are reading a book and really enjoying it. Let's say you are visualizing Denzel Washington in the lead role. Halfway through the book you learn you should have been visualizing George Clooney instead. Or vice-versa.

Neither of these choices is bad. But if you visualize one over the other then realize you've been visualizing incorrectly it's almost as if you have to start reading from the beginning again. And I would feel the same way if I were visualizing George Clooney and realized I should have been visualizing Brad Pitt instead. Or visualizing Denzel Washington when I should have been visualizing Don Cheadle.

This also holds true if I'm visualizing a brown-eyed brunette only to discover in the middle of the book or story that the character is actually a blue-eyed blond or a hazel-eyed redhead.

It's like replacing an actor on a soap opera with a completely different actor in mid-week, which has actually happened quote often over the years. Or switching an important player on a sports team with a different player in the middle of the game. Perspective changes when details of the character change.

It has nothing to do with the capabilities of the character. It has everything to do with the expectations of the reader.

The reader expects you to draw a picture of your character, at least enough of a picture so she or he can visualize the character almost as you see the character. The reader then trusts you to follow through with that picture and keep your character looking the same throughout the story.

You don't want to tell the reader what to see, but you do want to give the reader some idea of what you see.

Describing your character isn't building character. Building character is an entirely different discussion.

But character description is important to the reader. It enhances her or his imagination when it comes to visualizing the characters.

The reader experience is as important as the writer experience. It's the reader experience which gets the writer noticed and generates sales.

Four Building Blocks of Character

*Nobody is surprised that women writers accurately represent
male characters over and over again, no doubt because
everybody knows that women understand men much better than
vice-versa. ~Peter Straub*

Piece by piece a character is created. Not all at once, but in little increments so the reader keeps reading.

You want your characters to make an impression. You want them to be memorable. Use the following four building blocks to construct characters who will be memorable. They will also give your characters dimension and help the reader to see the character as you see her or him.

Physical Description

I have read many books lately that give very little description – or no description at all – of what the characters look like. Is this a trend?

You don't have to go into minute detail about a character's physique but at least cover the basics: height, weight, hair color, eye color, sex and ethnicity gives the reader an idea of the type of person they "see" as they read. This is the foundation upon which all other building blocks rest. You want it to be a strong foundation.

Is your protagonist male or female? How tall is your character? Is he thin or a little overweight? Is she blond and blue-eyed? Does she have any scars or tattoos? Does he have a twitch or a tic? Let your reader know what the character looks like from your perspective so she or he can develop a perspective of her or his own.

Personality

Without personality, a character exists only on the page. You want your characters to live vividly in the minds of your readers.

Is your character a good guy or a bad guy? Or somewhere in between? Is she or he brave? Compassionate? Evil? Greedy? Do they have any interesting habits? What are their shortcomings? Do they dress in a unique way? Do they have an unusual name? Establish personality early on and then build on them. Small bits and pieces keep the reader reading.

In Dean Koontz's *The Face* the character of Corky is a vivid and memorable character. He is an anarchist on a mission: to create chaos wherever he goes. He is introduced wearing a yellow rain slicker and putting racially-infested propaganda in strangers' mailboxes. His ultimate goal is to kidnap a Hollywood movie star's son, Frick (short for Aelfric). Frick is an intelligent boy who scoffs at his father's lifestyle and deals with his loneliness with witticisms. He also suffers from asthma. One read and you will never forget either of these two characters, not only because of their names but also for their unique personalities.

In the *Sword of Tilk Trilogy, Book Two: Strange Land*, Gregorio is a pirate who visits the Tilk Realm. But he's a pirate with style. His manner of dress is of primary note: a mustard-yellow jacket, a lime green tunic and tan breeches. Flamboyant colors are his trademark. Make no mistake, he's a ladies' man, but it is obvious he likes to be noticed. He wants to be remembered wherever he goes and he is remembered: vividly.

Mannerisms and Blemishes

While a picture-perfect character with blindingly white teeth may be the ideal protagonist, a character with a "blemish" can be twice as interesting. A character with a stuttering problem, a limp, an eye tic or any number of other small but significant details can make a hero out of a small and seemingly insignificant character.

Or it can elevate your main character above the level of hero. Equally, a blemish can heighten the vileness of an evil character. Don't go overboard and give all of your characters blemishes. One or two on occasion will do just fine.

For instance, in my current novel in progress, *Nero's Fiddle*, the character of Colt is a survivalist. He's a little on the gruff side, rarely smiles and has a constant eye tic as a result of PTSD. He also stands out because he makes his own beef jerky.

Mannerisms can also significantly enhance your character. Something such as a flip of the hair, a wink of an eye, scratching behind the ear, a vein that pops out in the center of the forehead when nervous or agitated: these little mannerisms can endear your character to the reader. Likewise, a habit of tapping a foot when impatient, tossing trash out the car window or being a non-stop chain smoker paints a picture of a character you don't want your readers to necessarily like but can still relate to.

In Harlan Coben's Myron Bolitar series, Myron has a best friend, Windsor Horne Lockwood III also known as Win. He is as pompous as his name sounds. Even if Mr. Coben didn't tell the reader Win is a rich philanthropist, the reader would know. The way he walks, talks, dresses, practices his golf swing in his office and steeples his fingers indicates he comes from money. Despite his attitude of superiority, Win is a likeable character. He is sort of Batman to Myron's Robin: Myron constantly gets into trouble, Win uses his money and connections to rescue him.

Challenge your characters

Think of some of the more popular action-packed movies you've seen. Indiana Jones comes immediately to mind. It seemed that Indiana took his foot out of one pile of crap only to place into another. If you want to keep the reader engaged, your characters must be faced with odds which seem insurmountable. You must devise a way for the character to overcome each obstacle he or she faces. How a character handles a particular situation says a lot about that character. It also makes an impression on the reader.

Building a character from the ground up requires diligence. You want the characters to be strong and make an impression, whether good or bad. Pay attention to your character as you visualize her or him. Then use the building blocks to construct your character and develop her or him into a three-dimensional person. Your readers will thank you.

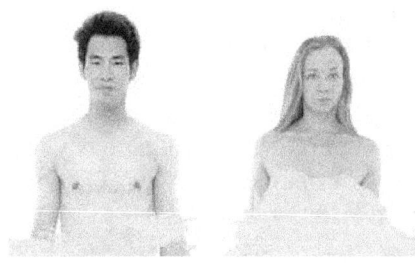

Naked Characters

When I was in third grade, I wrote a story and let one of my classmates read it. He was a chubby little kid much like myself but he was one of the nicer kids in my class.

After he read the story he handed it back to me. He'd rewritten it. At the time it kinda ticked me off; he did it in a rather mocking way.

Looking back, I see now he was trying to get a point across with humor.

I had created witty dialogue between two characters: one a mafia-type boss, the other his underling. I cannot for the life of me recall the dialogue or the subject of conversation.

What my friend did was poke fun at the fact that I had not included descriptions of clothing on my characters.

I hadn't given it that much thought. After all, everyone knows characters wear clothes, right?

Years later, I have come to realize that I do, at times, fall short when clothing my characters. It doesn't mean they're naked. It just means since I see them fully clothed in my head, I make the assumption the reader does as well.

It is erroneous thinking on my part. Just because I visualize my character wearing a pair of jeans and a t-shirt doesn't mean the reader won't see her or him in a sundress or a three-piece suit.

It's important to look at your characters closely. Analyze not only their physical description but the clothing she or he wears on their backs, as well.

Clothing description doesn't have to be that detailed, unless your character is a meticulous dresser or dresses gregariously like Gregorio in *Sword of Tilk Book Two: Strange Land*. Gregorio purposefully wears very colorful tunics and shirts to attract attention, even of the negative sort.

All it takes is a quick mention of "She was comfortable in ragged jeans and an old t-shirt" for the reader to see what your character is wearing.

Sometimes the clothing she or he wears can also help define the character or give a little insight into her or his personality. For instance, "He wore khakis and a Polo shirt even though it was Saturday," tells the reader this guy doesn't lounge around in his PJs even on the weekend. It gives the impression he may be too cultured for cut-off blue jeans and holey t-shirts.

By the same token, "She appeared in court wearing faded jeans with holes in the knees and a halter top with no bra" shows a degree of disrespect for authority, even though this manner of dress may seem the norm these days.

So, when you go in for the editing session, pay close attention to what your characters are wearing. Don't let them walk around naked. Get some clothes on 'em!

Tapping Into Your Own Personal Dexter

Writing a book is an adventure. To begin with it is a toy and an amusement. Then it becomes a mistress, then it becomes a master, then it becomes a tyrant. The last phase is that just as you are about to be reconciled to your servitude, you kill the monster and flint him to the public. ~Winston Churchill

As humans, we all have a dark side. Each of us is capable of experiencing anger, frustration and despair. As humans, we have (most of us anyway) learned to cope with this darker side and to not act upon our darker nature.

That darker side can come in handy for the writer.

I never thought I could be a fan of a serial killer. It goes against every moral fiber of my being. It wasn't until I stumbled across the audiobooks of Jeff Lindsay's Dexter series that I thought I would give them a try.

Dexter Morgan is actually a charming individual with his self-deprecating wit and his view of himself as a monster. Thanks to his foster father, Harry, Dexter found a way to satisfy his slaughterous tendencies by killing other serial killers, mainly those who commit murderous crimes against children.

Despite his claim that he has no conscience, Dexter has more of a conscious than most people I encounter on a daily basis. He is very much human, more so because he claims he is not than anything else. Even though, on occasion, Dexter allows his "Dark Passenger" to take control, his actions in between victims present him as just another ordinary guy. Sort of.

I wondered as I listened to those audiobooks (I've listened to several of them) how on earth Mr. Lindsay could create such a character?

That question lead to, how would I create such a character? Better still, how would I create a character who truly has no conscience?

It isn't as easy as it seems to create a vile character who performs despicable acts. At least I don't find it so easy. It's a little frightening to imagine what I could do if I had no conscience. (Hey, I'm a Scorpio so my personality could go either way.)

As I pondered how I was going to create my character Desdemona in the *Sword of Tilk Trilogy* and make her someone people could really hate, some guy cut me off in traffic.

I am not prone to road rage though I understand the inclination. It's difficult not to react when some idiot does something stupid in traffic that could result in fatalities.

When it happened and after I finished letting loose a string of expletives that would do a sailor proud, a light bulb went off over my head. (This doesn't happen often so when it does I tend to pay attention.)

All those emotions the incident conjured could be applied to an evil character.

Better yet, use that bottomless imagination of mine and what I would do *if I could get away with it*.

That is a big IF.

Remove the barriers of conscience, punishment and retribution and allow your imagination to take you where it will. Do keep in mind that these acts are not something you would actually *do*, even if you could get away with it.

Then project it onto your evil character(s).

The evil witch Desdemona (from the Sword of Tilk Trilogy) must kill her own mother.

Harming a parent, a child or a pet are three of the most evil, vile and contemptible acts any human being can perform. I hope there is a special place in hell for those people who perform them.

In order to write the scene where Desdemona performs this act, I had to imagine a person I held beneath contempt.

Face it: there is someone in almost every person's life that is held beneath contempt. It is virtually impossible to live in this world without feeling that way about somebody.

The guy in traffic isn't one of them.

Be that as it may, I visualized Desdemona performing the murderous deed to this person.

And, yes, I must confess, I fantasized about doing it myself in an effort to experience what it might feel like.

Mr. Lindsay did an excellent job of portraying the Dexter Morgan character. But he actually made Dexter likeable.

A noble thing to be sure but if you want your characters to be evil – truly evil – then you have to put yourself in their shoes. Imaginatively, not literally, of course.

We each have a Dexter inside: That part of us which wishes to get even, get ahead no matter what it takes, or simply would like to see others suffer when they deserve it. Deny it all you like, it's there. It's just a good thing the majority of us has a conscience that keeps that dark side in check.

The dark side is not a place I wish to dwell. It wouldn't be comfortable to live there round the clock.

But tapping into it when needed is a vital part of the writing process.

Writing Stuff

*A person is a fool to become a writer. His only compensation is
absolute freedom. He has no master except his own soul, and that,
I am sure, is why he does it. ~ Roald Dahl*

That Nit-Picky Little Apostrophe

O, apostrophe, O, apostrophe
What would we do without thee?
Your contractions, how they shine!
Your placement is divine!
Two words you do conjoin,
To create one word to conform,
You bend to show possession,
And always make concession,
When deleting a letter or two,
O, what would the English language
Be without you?

Enough of the *Ode to the Apostrophe*. Let's take a closer look at this little character.

An apostrophe is used to denote a contraction – the combining of two words – and possession – when something belongs to someone. It is also used from time to time to shorten a word into slang or when letters are deleted from a word.

By far the most confused contraction ever is **it's**. This word is a contraction for the two words "**it is**." However, it is forever and over being misused.

My second grade teacher, Miss Myrtle, taught us to read the entire sentence in which the word appears. If you can read the sentence with "it is" and it makes sense, use the apostrophe.

For example: "**It's** a foregone conclusion...." Read the sentence as "**It is** a foregone conclusion..." It makes sense so the apostrophe is in the right place. This is a contraction and requires an apostrophe.

If the sentence read thusly does not make sense, there is no apostrophe.

For instance: "The bird flew into *its* nest." Read as, "The bird flew into *it is* nest." This doesn't make sense so there is no apostrophe. This is the possessive form and does not require an apostrophe.

When letters are intentionally deleted from a word, there should be an apostrophe. If you want to shorten the word chocolate to choc'late, the apostrophe is placed where the letter would normally be.

"Them" is a popular word to shorten. Times like this, the apostrophe ends up turned backwards. Technically, it is incorrect. Yet I have seen the backwards apostrophe in television commercials, magazine ads, and books published by big name publishing houses. And, of course, the Internet is littered with backwards apostrophes.

There is a simple way to make sure the apostrophe is correct in this instance. When you shorten the word "them" to **'em** (**'em** is how it normally shows up), and you want that apostrophe to be facing the correct way, you first type a letter, any letter, then type the apostrophe and the rest of the word. Go back and delete that first letter and *voila*! your apostrophe is turned the correct way. (And the word is pronounced *vwahla* and not *wahla* as I have heard it often mispronounced. I'm sure the French would appreciate the correct pronunciation).

I will admit I am as guilty as anyone else for misplacing an apostrophe on occasion. But I strive to make certain I'm putting it in its place.

Granted, it's a nit-picky little thing to worry about. But the apostrophe is one of those details writers need to pay attention to. Because readers pay attention.

Is He Staring at Me?
Depends on How You Look At It

For your born writer, nothing is so healing as the realization that he has come upon the right word. ~Catherine Drinker Bowen

In several books I have read recently, I've noticed the word "look" and its myriad of connotations take something of a beating.

Characters stare when all they need do is look. They gaze when they should glare. And they glimpse when they should gaze.

Word usage can be confusing, especially if you don't give serious consideration to what an action or actions mean. But you want to give the reader the right idea and that means using the correct word.

Consider these words and their definitions (courtesy of www.dictionary.com):

Look: to turn one's eyes toward something or in some direction in order to see.

Glance: to look quickly or briefly.

Stare: to gaze fixedly and intently, especially with the eyes wide open.

Glare: to stare with a fiercely or angrily piercing look.

Gaze: to look steadily and intently, as with great curiosity, interest, pleasure, or wonder.

Gape: to stare with open mouth, as in wonder.

Glimpse: a very brief, passing look, sight, or view.

A glimpse is less than a glance. A glance is less than everything else.

To glare at someone implies anger or irritation.

To stare is intentional; looking at someone without blinking but with concentration.

Gaze and gape are similar in that both words apply pleasant wonder.

To look is just that: to look at something.

I feel compelled to differentiate between these words because they are not interchangeable. Each word has a different meaning and denotes a different facial expression.

For instance, in a few books I recently read, the sentence "He stared at her" kept popping up. However, the situations didn't warrant staring. "He looked at her" would have sufficed in most cases. There was one instance where "He glared at her" would have been more appropriate because the male character was angry with the female character.

Each of these words carries the weight of emotion.

Staring suggests the person staring is not pleased with the subject being stared at.

Example: He stared at her for her ludicrous suggestion.

On the flip side, staring can also mean a pleasant obsession.

Example: He stared at the dancer onstage, drinking her in.

Either way, the word staring suggests varying degrees of obsession. It also suggests surprise and fear.

To glance at something is to quickly look at something then return attention to the matter at hand. Returning the attention is understood when using the word glance.

Example: She glanced at the letter in his hand and continued reading her book.

To catch a glimpse of something is to not even get a good look at it.

Example: She glimpsed movement from the corner of her eye.

Gaze and gape are similar, but to gape at something includes an open mouth, thus enhancing the emotion of wonder.

Example: He gazed at the pool of water shimmering in the moonlight.

Example: She gaped at the starship standing before her ready for launch.

As stated before, I point these out because when reading these words I expect a certain emotion to accompany them. When the male character was staring at the female character, I really couldn't understand why he would be staring with wide-open eyes. The male character was not surprised, fearful nor upset or angry. Just looking at the female character, maybe as though she had lost her mind, but just looking at her, all the same.

It may seem a little on the picky side. But when I am reading a book and visualizing the characters, I feel disappointed when the facial expression in the book doesn't relate to the one I see in my head. Not because I cannot visualize but because the improper word for the facial expression was used.

When setting your characters up to look, stare, gaze or glance be mindful of the situation at hand, how the characters feel and how they relate to one another. You want to send the right message to the reader so the reader can experience what the characters are experiencing.

You want to leave the reader with wide-eyed wonder.

Write it Like You Tell It

If I do not write to empty my mind, I go mad.
~George Gordon Byron

I am asked from time to time, in various ways, "How do I write this story?" This question is usually posed regarding a writer writing the story of another person.

I answer simply: "Write it like you tell it."

The answer is simple. Actually doing it is a little more challenging.

If the story you're writing is about someone else, get as many details from them as possible. Record your conversations with them for reference. Familiarize yourself with their story until you know it verbatim just remember to write it in your own words except for dialogue. You'll want to use the other person's style of speech for that.

First, determine the scope and classification of your story. Is it biographical or a memoir? Is it based on a true story or inspired by a true story? Is it fact-based?

Here is the difference between all those terms:

Biographical: a written account of another person's life

Fact-based: Based on or concerned with true events or experiences

Based on a true story: some of the events are based on real life occurrences but the writers have made up a lot of it

Inspired by a true story: More of the story is made up by the writer than actually told by the person it pertains to.

Memoir: a historical account or biography written from personal knowledge or special sources.

Each of these genres requires different steps.

Biographies and memoirs require extensive research and investigation. It is necessary to interview people who know the person whose story you are writing to corroborate the person's story. It may also entail digging up any articles that may be available regarding the story.

Inspired by a true story may not have a single grain of truth in it. To be inspired means you feel compelled to do something based upon something else but it doesn't have to include that something else.

Based on a true story is basically a true story with imagined embellishments. The events themselves may be true but how the person got from point A to point B may be fictionalized. If you weren't there you have to imagine what it was like and that's where the embellishment comes in.

Fact-based is just that: it requires more fact than fiction. Some fictionalizing must occur, but the facts need to be on record.

Now that you have determined which avenue you wish to follow you have an idea of how much work is ahead of you. You can also use the terms as taglines for your story which can be a good selling point for it.

Start by writing down the story just as if you were telling it to another person. No holds barred. Anything and everything you would say. Don't worry about clean up or how it sounds in this initial stage. You want to make sure to get as many of your ideas, thoughts, and feelings down on paper as possible.

Once you have completed this task, go through your story searching for places which need any enhancements, fictionalizing, explanation, details or any other changes. Gather more information if you must.

Do whatever rewriting or editing you need to do, again, as though you were verbalizing the story to someone.

Now walk away. No, no don't abandon the work. Give yourself a few days or even a week before going back to read the story again. You're going to need that rest to gather your strength. Because now it's time to get tough.

Read the story as though someone else had written it. What do you like about the story? What would you change?

A little time and space away from the story will give you a fresh perspective. It enables you to look at the writing with a more objective eye. There may be aspects you're not happy with and need to work on. There may be other enhancements you didn't think of in the initial writing. You may need to do more investigation to strengthen the story.

This may be a process you'll want to repeat until you feel confident you have done the best job you can possibly do. You're writing another person's story so you want to honor them by doing your best.

Once you feel the story is done, your work is not. Now comes the clean-up. This is where you go through and make sure all I's are dotted and T's are crossed. Make sure verb usage is correct and consistent, i.e. past or present. Check grammar, punctuation and spelling. Make certain the story flows smoothly and coherently.

Get other people to read the story. Have the person the story is about read it. Listen to all feedback with an open mind and objectivity. They're giving you honest feedback. Respect that. Analyze it to see how it can help you improve your writing.

Once all is said and done, not only will the voice of the person you're writing about be heard, so will yours.

Writing Around the Details

*Writing a novel is a terrible experience, during which the hair
often falls out and the teeth decay. I'm always irritated by people
who imply that writing fiction is an escape from reality. It is a
plunge into reality and it's very shocking to the system.*
~Flannery O'Connor

Some details simply aren't necessary. You don't have to
provide a detailed summary of injuries sustained to characters,
don't have to be or consult with a doctor for a prognosis. Those
details can sometimes be more detrimental to a story than helpful
to the reader.

A prime example of this is Jeff Lindsay's *Dexter By Design*.

For those not familiar with Lindsay's Dexter series: Dexter is
a serial killer who kills serial killers. He mostly targets those
guilty of crimes against children, primarily pedophiles who kill
children. He is also a blood splatter analyst for the Miami Police
Department. His foster sister, Deborah, also works for the Miami
Police Department.

In *Dexter By Design*, Dexter and Deborah pay a visit to the
home of a suspect. Deborah is stabbed in the process and
hospitalized.

Not once throughout the ordeal does Lindsay go into detail
about Deborah's injuries. The only thing the reader knows is that
"she lost a lot of blood."

No medical jargon. No technical mumbo-jumbo. No lengthy
explanations about where the knife penetrated, what organs (if
any) that may have been affected and no platitudes about how
lucky Deborah was.

Instead, Lindsay focuses on the real issue: the relationship
between Deborah and Dexter.

Deborah recently discovered Dexter's secret life and she was
processing her feelings about the matter.

Dexter was processing how he felt about his sister. Feelings are something Dexter is always processing, whether he believes he has them or not.

There was already enough going on in the novel without it getting bogged down with medical details regarding Deborah's injury. Going into those details would have been tedious instead of enlightening. Rather than have the reader stumble through the medical vernacular, Lindsay keeps the important stuff in the forefront while using Deborah's injury as background drama.

Details about her injury simply aren't necessary. It is enough to know that Deborah has sustained a potentially life-threatening injury and even more important is how Dexter reacts to it and feels about it. Details about the injury itself would have added insult (pun intended).

It is the foremost job of the writer to keep the story moving, keep the reader interested. Had Mr. Lindsay insisted upon including medical and technical details about Deborah's injury, not one of those details would have been pertinent to the story. It would have just been information the reader had to slog through to get to the next interesting part.

This doesn't mean you should forego any research that needs to be done. There are details that are imperative you know something about.

For instance, in the novel I am currently working on, I need to learn more about guns. This will require hands-on research: visiting a firing range, talking to people who are gun enthusiasts and probably handling and shooting one as well.

I'm not crazy about guns. They scare me. I've never held one unless you count the childhood water gun. It is imperative that I overcome this, steel my nerves and do that research. But one of my characters is a superior markswoman (that's right, I said woman). She's gonna know her gun, know it well and know how to handle it. This is an important detail in the novel and the research must be done.

Weigh the importance of your details to your reader. Must they know that a conduit is not only a means of conveying water it also denotes a means of access? Do they really need to know the minute details of an injury or would it suffice they know it is life-threatening? Do they need to know the exact route to get to the buried treasure or is it more important what the characters endure to get there?

While the details can be interesting if they don't move the story along or make a poignant point it may be best to write around them. Sometimes the how and the why of a thing isn't as important as how the people affected deal with it.

It isn't that details don't matter, they do. As long as you expend the time and energy on the really important details.

Using Backstory to Enhance the Story

Ideas are like rabbits. You get a couple and learn how to handle them, and pretty soon you have a dozen. ~John Steinbeck

Delving into a character's past can be a complicated, tricky endeavor. Spreading details throughout the story keeps it interesting and keeps the reader reading.

A method to tell the past of my characters which worked well for me is using the backstory.

I was inspired to use this method by the television series "Once Upon A Time." The show is very adept at using the backstory of fairy tale characters to present them in a more realistic and imaginative light.

In *Sword of Tilk Book One: Worlds Apart* and *Book Two: Strange Land* I used the backstory told by Jean, grandmother of the twin Queens. The events related in her narratives were relevant to situations currently faced by the characters. Both narratives were a story within the story.

In *Book Three: At Sword's End*, I used the memories of evil witch Desdemona to enlighten the reader about the backstory. Desdemona also used "earth memories" which she could conjure at will.

In *Nero's Fiddle*, Captain Beverly Mossberg had nightmares due to PTSD. Her nightmares reflected an incident which occurred during her tour in the Gulf War. A little of the incident was revealed with each nightmare; some nightmares were more horrific than what actually happened. The nightmares provided the backstory.

In the *Sword of Tilk Trilogy*, including the backstories was instrumental to the story itself. The Tilk family history was an essential part of the story illustrating how those past events affect current events. It also displayed the characters at a different point in their lives and explained the people they became.

In *Nero's Fiddle*, the nightmares not only provided backstory, they also served as one of the symptoms of Post Traumatic Stress Disorder.

Creating a backstory in each and every novel isn't necessary. It can add a layer of intrigue to your characters as well as your plot. But use it wisely. If it enhances the characters, moves the story along or affects an important plot point, include it.

The backstory can help you as a writer to better understand your characters or the central point of your novel. It can also enhance the reader's experience and give her or him a more full understanding of your characters.

It can also be fun, delving into the character's past and/or psyche.

If it's fun for you, it will be fun for the reader.

Writing the Slow Build

There are three rules for writing a novel. Unfortunately, no one knows what they are. ~W. Somerset Maugham

A common mistake made by beginning writers is trying to tell the entire story in the first chapter. Or even in the first paragraph.

By giving your novel the "slow build" you give the reader a better opportunity to be enchanted with your story and your characters.

A prime example of this slow build process is Lindsay Buroker's *The Emperor's Edge* series.

While most authors write a single novel, Ms. Buroker takes her readers and her characters through a series of seven books (thus far). This affords her the luxury of building on her characters with each series entry. She has mastered the slow build.

I'll use the character of Akstyr as an illustration.

When we first meet Akstyr he is in the stockade for practicing magic. The Turgonian Empire denies the very existence of magic. Anyone practicing it is punished. Amaranthe Lokdon, the heroin of the series, enlists Akstyr's help in a plot to thwart the assassination of Emperor Sespian.

From the moment we meet him, Akstyr displays contempt toward everyone and everything, with the exception of studying magic. One wonders why he chose to throw his lot in with this band of miscreants. He keeps himself distanced from everyone in the group, even plotting to turn one of them in for the bounty. He's one of those characters you want to like but his attitude and his actions leave you shaking your head.

Once we meet Akstyr's mother in *Blood and Betrayal* (Book 5) we begin to understand the young man's attitude. We also realize his attitude is a defense mechanism: he uses it to protect himself against getting hurt.

We also find out he cares more than he lets on.

By presenting him as a lackadaisical character Buroker piques the reader's interest about him while also tweaking just a touch of frustration with him.

Once his true nature is revealed, all is forgiven. Almost all.

It's almost like knowing a real person.

The slow build process Ms. Buroker spans over several novels can be achieved in one. It's all about timing: When, where and how you choose to divulge the essential aspects of your character so your reader gets to know that character gradually. Just like getting to know a real person.

Give the reader just enough to keep them wanting more.

Writing the Action-Packed Thriller

The writer's job is to get the main character up a tree,
and then once they are up there, throw rocks at them.
~Vladimir Nabokov

So you'd like to write an action-packed thriller.

I highly recommend reading James Rollins' Sigma Force series. Any book in the series will give you an idea of the best way to tackle this genre.

Meet Sigma Force, a covert underground government agency whose main task is protecting the world from global threats. Literally underground: the facility is beneath the Smithsonian Institution (fictionally, of course).

The Sigma Force team barely has time to catch its collective breath between one challenge and another. But even the time between challenges is peppered with drama and interesting historical knowledge.

Each Sigma Force operative has her or his own unique area of scientific intelligence:

Painter Crowe: micro-surveillance computer engineering.
Grayson Pierce: biology and physics.
Monk Kokkalis: forensic medicine and biotechnology.
Kathryn Bryant: intelligence services and coordination.
Lisa Cummings: human physiology marine sciences.
Joe Kowalski: demolitions and occasional comic relief.
Seichan: former assassin for The Guild, Sigma Force's nemesis, now part of Sigma.

They are a close-knit team headed by Director Painter Crowe of Native American Heritage.

Rollins fuses historical spiritual facts and rumors with modern scientific knowledge and concepts. He accomplishes a balance between the two without falling into religious rhetoric or scientific geekdom. It gives the reader something to think about. At the very least some things in the Sigma Force novels may prompt you to do a Google search to see how much of the novel is based on fact. (You would be surprised).

Many authors feel the need to fill the gaps between events with thoughtful passages or snippets of description. Rollins writes the Sigma Force novels with a timeline: he dates and time stamps each action sequence guaranteeing there are no lulls in between each set of action. The characters don't have time to dwell on whatever occurred between events and the reader is too busy keeping up to wonder.

There are times when Rollins literally has only a few minutes' time from one scene to another. You'd be amazed what a character can accomplish in the span of only a few minutes. This makes for very fast-paced reading and a sure-fire way to keep the pages turning. It practically guarantees reader satisfaction.

That is the unique aspect of the action/thriller genre. Details found in other genres aren't as essential. Emotional aspects of the characters are important – and still accounted for – but it isn't necessary to delve as deeply into them. The focus is on the action and keeping it moving to keep the reader interested.

This can sometimes work to the writer's advantage. Writing emotional aspects of characters can sometimes be difficult and, quite honestly, draining. It's a nice change of pace to concentrate on what the characters are doing and not so much on what they are feeling.

The reader develops a like or dislike for the characters based upon the actions each one takes. That doesn't mean the reader doesn't get emotionally involved. The emotional descriptions of Rollins' characters are vivid but succinct, displayed mostly with actions. This better impacts the emotional response of the reader, sometimes achieving a more heightened response than a lengthy description of what the character feels.

Each action the characters take continues developing the emotional reaction in the reader as well as developing the character.

Of course, it depends upon the reader as well. Writing action without lengthy emotional description would probably not appeal to someone who reads romance novels.

But if you're interested in writing a thriller, pick up any of James Rollins' Sigma Force novels. Read it the first time to enjoy it. Read it the second, third, fourth and fifth times to study it.

Granted, there are a plethora of authors who write in the thriller genre; James Patterson and Dan Brown come to mind. Rollins is my personal favorite.

Leaving the reader exhausted is a good thing: it's an experience she or he will not soon forget.

Chapter Endings that Turn Pages

*Every word a woman writes changes the story of the world,
revises the official version. ~Carolyn See*

Sometimes it's difficult to know where and how to end a chapter. The writing is flowing and everything is coming together. But you need to change the scene and start a new chapter and you're not sure how to end this one.

Two sure-fire ways to end a chapter that keep me turning the page are: humor and tension.

I like characters who exhibit a sense of humor even in the most dire of situations. The master of blending humor with tension is Dean Koontz.

This ending of Chapter Five in Koontz's *By the Light of the Moon* is a prime example of cutting the tension with humor while maintaining the drama:

As Dylan quickly cut away the remaining restraints, the jigsaw junkie – now locking pieces in the picture at a frenetic pace that even methamphetamine could not have precipitated – altered his nonsense chant: "Deedle-doodle-diddle."

"I feel a pressure in my middle."

"Deedle-doodle-diddle."

"I think I have to piddle."

This scenario occurs after Dylan and his brother Shepherd, who suffers Asperger Syndrome, have been given shots of some unidentified stuff by a man resembling a mad scientist. Putting together a jigsaw puzzle at top speed and uttering "Deedle-doodle-diddle" is Shep's way of dealing with the situation. The rhymed response is Dylan's.

The tension-laden chapter ending is a foolproof attention-grabber, practically guaranteeing the reader won't put the book down.

This excerpt from my work in progress, *Nero's Fiddle* demonstrates:

Bev's instincts were in high gear; that tingling sensation along the base of her neck had her attentive.

Below the sounds of birdsong and rustling undergrowth, she heard a noise that didn't belong. It was a sound with which she was very familiar: The click of the hammer of a weapon.

She slowly turned her head to the right.

And found herself face to face with the business end of a double-barrel shotgun.

This chapter comes to a close on a scene which begs the reader to turn the page and keep reading. It also occurs in a point in the novel when the reader is well invested in this character and her cause.

Ending a chapter at a point where the character displays humor in the face of adversity (thereby displaying a strong character in my opinion), or ending it with the character facing a dangerous situation is certain to keep your readers reading. And loving what they read.

Inspiring the Reader

If there's a book that you want to read, but it hasn't been written yet, then you must write it. ~Toni Morrison

You want to inspire a reader to read your book and tell everyone else about it. But that's not the only way you want to inspire the reader.

You want to inspire the reader to think: think about what you've written what your characters have endured and possibly how it could affect their lives.

You do this by having characters who change their own lives.

For instance, if your character begins as a struggling musician and ends up winning a Grammy, facing and overcoming every challenge in between, your reader may be inspired to follow her or his own creative career.

Barbara Neely is the lead character in my *Sword of Tilk Trilogy. In Book One: Worlds Apart*, she struggles to take care of herself, her daughter and her foster grandmother; she doesn't even have the confidence to stand up to her boss. By *Book Three: At Sword's End* she is quite comfortable being one of the Queens of the Tilk Realm. And it was quite the journey she made to reach that point.

You inspire the reader by showing her or him what is possible. Providing them with the steps a character takes to reach her or his destination may very well give the reader ideas about how to reach her or his own destinations.

Your writing may serve to inspire others to write.

Even though I have been writing since the age of ten, I hadn't attempted writing a full length novel. My imagination certainly at work doing hours of daydreaming. But I never connected my daydreams to the possibility of making novels out of them.

If you don't know what Maladaptive Daydreaming is I'll tell you in a nutshell: it is daydreaming to the point of excess, almost to the point of not being able to distinguish reality from daydreams.

I've been doing that since the age of four.

Be that as it may, I one day picked up two Dean Koontz novels: *By the Light of the Moon* and *One Door Away From Heaven*.

Reading them changed my perspective on my daydreams. Because both books sounded like something I would have daydreamed about.

From that point on, I have been writing whatever comes into my head.

You see, maladaptive daydreamers, such as myself, are capable of creating and developing very elaborate and extensive daydreams. The daydreams cast about in my mind are vivid and rich with details. All I have to do is translate them onto paper.

Some people call it daydreaming. I call it visualization with a purpose.

Not everything you write is going to inspire everyone. But if you inspire even only ONE person, you are doing what you are meant to do.

Errors? Sew Whut?

Fiction is, after all, an alternate reality; a reality which spans worlds, fills the void between worlds and creates worlds filled with promise and vision. ~Pen

The misspelling is intentional.

I hate coming across errors in books. I hate it even more when I come across errors in my own books. And even more when other people come across them.

I'm not upset with other people for finding them: I'm upset with myself for *not* finding them.

I do everything I possibly can to catch everything but a few things do get by me.

I would love to have a professional proofreader and editor go over my work. But I'm poor. That's with a capital POOR, especially by today's standards. It doesn't matter how "inexpensive" the fees are claimed to be, I cannot afford them.

Family and friends aren't interested in reading the genre of books I write.

Therefore, I do the best I can.

But here's the thing: I have read more books than I care to think about that have been published by *traditional publishing houses* that are chock full of errors.

I point them out here not in an attempt to embarrass anyone, nor to gloat. I merely wish to point out how commonplace errors have become. The authors whose works I cite are among my favorites. However, I will refrain from mentioning names or citing book titles.

While reading the work of a prolific author whose works I particularly enjoy, I came across several errors in the book. I was surprised when I stumbled across them because the works of this author are among the most error-free I have read.

This did not diminish my reading experience but it did lead me to wonder what happened. Had the author's personal editor retired, forcing him to find a new, less experienced editor? If his publishing house has a professional editor on staff, was this editor also less experienced? Or perhaps too harried to catch everything?

That is the job of professional proofreaders and editors, to catch and correct errors in raw manuscripts.

Another prolific and popular author was gearing up for the release of his latest novel in the summer of 2014. He made the first few chapters available for download. Eagerly, I downloaded and read those first chapters.

And found three errors in the first nineteen pages.

Did this deter me from buying the book? Hell, no. I could hardly wait to get my hands on it.

Most traditional publishing houses no longer keep professional proofreaders and editors on staff in the interest of saving a few bucks. Granted, printing costs are exorbitant and the economy is brutal. But must the integrity of professional publishing suffer?

Even those publishing houses which retain editors hire those with less experience: they can offer them less pay.

Ergo, errors make their way into books published by those big name houses.

When it comes to self-publishing, errors abound. In many cases, this will deter sales but there are exceptions.

One independent author who churns out books on an almost weekly basis enjoys healthy sales. I particularly enjoy one of her series even though it contains numerous errors. She acknowledges an editor in each book. But it must have been a less-experienced editor.

Again, those errors do not diminish the reading experience. The characters are engaging as are the storylines of each installment in the series. I'm overwhelmed by the creativity of this author. Her creativity helps to inspire my own.

The errors in her books don't deter sales. But she has worked hard for many years to establish a following and those followers are loyal. Most of her posted reviews are positive, though a few do point out the glaring misspellings and incorrect word usage.

As one last example, a very popular, ahem, vampire series is littered with errors. Yet this series is in the top ten books read and all installments were made into blockbuster movies.

Truth be told, there are so many misspellings and incorrect grammar usage, both in advertising and on the Internet, that the majority of people no longer notice errors. Many are not bothered by the incorrect usage of to, too, or two, their, they're or there or its as opposed to it's.

Make no mistake there are plenty of people who comb books for the specific purpose of finding errors. And they take a certain macabre glee in pointing out each and every one.

It is a never-ending – and losing, I might add – battle to educate the reading public. Especially younger generations, so accustomed to abbreviated text messaging they no longer know how to spell the words they're abbreviating.

Future generations won't recognize over half the errors in today's published books.

You might think at this point that leaving errors in your book is acceptable. You would be wrong.

By all means, clean up that book prior to publishing, whether you're going the self-publishing route or trying to get a book deal.

Read it carefully. Take a break of a few days or even a week and read it again. Remember that Spellcheck doesn't catch everything. But a reader who finds mistakes annoying certainly will.

Get someone, anyone who is willing, to read your book for feedback as well as helping you locate any errors in your writing. If you can afford to pay someone to proofread and edit your book, by all means do so. Barter if you can but do everything humanly possible to clean up that book.

Otherwise, risk coming under fire for the mistakes you made. Readers can be unforgiving.

If someone insists upon telling you each and every error they found in your book, just smile and nod knowing you are not alone.

Also keep in mind one HUGE advantage self-publishing has over traditional publishing: An independent author can always make any necessary corrections and upload the corrected file.

Errors in traditionally published books stand for all time.

Tools To Help You Write Better

You must stay drunk on writing so reality cannot destroy you.
~Ray Bradbury

The Soundtrack of Writing

No tears in the writer, no tears in the reader. No surprise in the writer, no surprise in the reader. ~Robert Frost

Like any good movie, a good book requires the proper background music. Writing with a soundtrack can help boost creativity and productivity.

What type of book are you writing?

Murder mystery
Science Fiction
Western
Romance

Each of these categories has appropriate background music. Think of the last Science Fiction or Romance movie you watched. What type of music was in the background? Was it dramatic? Was it light-hearted? Did it enhance your movie-going experience? Whether you paid attention to the music or not, some of it probably stayed with you.

For that reason, using background music while writing will make a book stay with a reader.

Choose the Music for Your Writing

It stands to reason that Country Music may be best suited for writing a Western novel. But don't rule out listening to Garth Brooks or Trisha Yearwood for Romance. Likewise, consider Classical for Science Fiction or a Murder Mystery.

Some of the music of Phillip Glass is well-suited for stories of vampires, ghosts or the darker side of human nature. Many of his instrumentals are short and concise but have a deep sense of foreboding.

The Book Chooses the Music

There are times when music fits perfectly with whatever you're working on.

For instance, for the *Sword of Tilk Trilogy*, all I heard was Pat Benatar.

Invincible accompanied my protagonist as she rode her black steed, Galindore, to rescue her daughter

Le Bel Age was background for every sword fight

All Fired Up was instrumental in helping my protagonist face her worst fears

The strength and the wherewithal in the Benatar tunes helped to draw out the strength in my characters. My protagonist in the Trilogy lacked self-confidence in the first installment. By the final book, she was very comfortable with herself being the Queen of a Realm.

Song Lyric Interference

Afraid song lyrics may interfere with your writing? Give Classical compositions a try. Many movies utilize Classical music to set the tone. Those Classical pieces serve just as well when writing. A number of Classical pieces are available for free download at www.amazon.com . The music of Mozart, Beethoven, Bach, et al, are timeless pieces and capable of evoking a myriad of emotions and visualizations.

It's About the Reader, Too

Using music to set the tone for writing doesn't just benefit the writer. It also serves to enhance the reading experience.

Like music enhances a movie, the music you hear in your head while writing will enhance every aspect of your writing. It will attune you to dialogue, character development, emotions and descriptions. The stronger and more realistic the visualization, the better you will write it.

The reader will not be able to hear what you hear. She or he may have an altogether different soundtrack in mind while reading. Or no soundtrack at all.

Regardless of what the reader hears or doesn't hear, use your favorite tunes to create. The important thing is that you use the music to reach your best writing potential.

Any tool a writer can use to enhance her or his writing is invaluable. Create a Playlist that will enhance your writing experience. It is sure to flow over into the reading experience as well.

This article first appeared on the Savvy Writers website:
http://bit.ly/1nQntx2

Audiobooks Can Help You Write Better

No black woman writer in this culture can write "too much."
Indeed, no woman writer can write "too much"... No woman has
ever written enough. ~bell hooks

How can listening to an audiobook help improve your writing?

Truth be told it never occurred to me that it could be a useful tool. Until one day while working on the *Sword of Tilk Trilogy* I realized I could hear the narrator of the audiobook I was listening to at work read the book as I wrote it.

This gave me pause.

I visualize each scene and snippet of dialogue before and as I write it. It had never occurred to me to hear it as it might be read for an audiobook.

I found that I liked it.

Most audiobook compilations hire professional readers to create the audiobook. These readers have years of experience under their belts. Much like actors bring characters to life, these readers breathe life into a book simply by reading it.

Hearing someone else read what I wrote helped me to determine where the emphasis lay. It helped me find areas which needed strengthening as well as areas which might require a lighter touch.

It gave greater voice to my characters. Just as visualizing helps to describe them, listening to the reader in my head helped me hear the cadence and rhythm of their voices. This in turn helped me see and better describe their facial expressions and body movements.

It was also beneficial in writing action and descriptive passages. A good, professional audiobook reader is capable of intensifying those moments with as much emotion and drama as when reading dialogue.

~ 92 ~

Check out some of these audiobooks at your local library:

The Passage by Justin Cronin, read by actor Edward Hermann

Any of the Dexter series, most read by author Jeff Lindsay himself

Any of James Rollins' Sigma Force novels

Check to see if some of your favorite books or authors are available on audiobook. Listen to them, pay attention to the cadence and rhythm of the reader's voice. Then imagine that voice reading your book as you write it.

"Hearing" the book as it would be read may help you determine where and what to emphasize, may help you create dialogue and description that you might have otherwise overlooked.

It brings yet another dimension to writing and breathing life into your writing. That which heightens your writing experience will be passed on to the reader experience.

Promotion and Marketing

You can't think yourself out of a writing block; you have to write yourself out of a thinking block. ~John Rogers

Promotion and Marketing

You fail only if you stop writing. ~Ray Bradbury

Congratulations. Your book is complete. You have it uploaded to Amazon and/or Smashwords.

But how do you get it noticed? How do you let people know it's available, what it's about, why they should read it?

Of all the aspects of writing, I find this the most difficult.

I'm not a social butterfly. I am by no means an expert at promotion, especially when it comes to promoting myself. I look at promotion and marketing much the same as I view computers: it is a necessary evil. As long as the computer understands I have no misgivings about taking a sledgehammer to it, I understand I must learn to use it.

Kinda hard to take a sledgehammer to promotion and marketing.

But perhaps it could be approached with the attitude of a sledgehammer: strong, invincible and with the intention of making an impact.

All the advice I have read regarding P&M suggests that writers think about it before they begin writing.

Let's be honest here. If you are a natural-born, dyed-in-the-wool writer, all you ever think about is writing. Right? This statement may not be true for some, but for me it's carved in stone.

Switching gears from writing to P&M isn't easy. It's like climbing up a steep hill in reverse.

Nevertheless, it is necessary. And though I am still in the throes of learning about it, I will share what I have learned thus far.

Start with acquiring local support. Make a list of media outlets around you as well as book stores, libraries and other places where you can do readings and/or book signings. Research each and every item on that list. By research, I don't mean just find a contact name and email address. Connect with them. Compliment a reporter or editor on her or his work. Interact with them on social media. Get to know them and let them get to know you before you start pitching stuff to them. It doesn't guarantee you'll get an interview or exposure, but it will help smooth the way.

Set up a Media Kit on your website as well as create a hard copy packet.

For the website version check out the online Media Kit for author Stephanie Sloane (http://bit.ly/VPKWH9). It is professional, comprehensive, aesthetically pleasing and interesting to read as well as easy to find.

For your physical Media Kit packet use high quality paper, professional photographs and a high end folder in which to keep the information. Keep several Media Kits in your car in the event you are asked to provide one in person.

The most basic Media Kit needs the following:

Bio
List of Publications
Fact Sheet
FAQs
Color and B&W Photos (of you, the author)
Interview Questions and Answers
Any Testimonials or Reviews you have

An expanded Media Kit may include:

Review copies of your book – autographed
News angles if your book has any
Any speaking or book signing engagements you have set up
Reviews and awards, if any

It's a good idea to also include an electronic copy of your Media Kit in CD Rom

Another helpful suggestion is you may want to make a high quality copy of your book cover to paste onto the cover of your Media Kit folder. It's eye-catching and sets you a little apart from everyone else.

Now you get to work on some other things today's independent authors are told they must do and have in their promotion and marketing skill set: branding and platform.

Don't Brand Me

You're a writer, the 'normal' ship sailed without you long ago.
~Terri Main

No matter who you are or what you are trying to accomplish, you're being told you must develop a "brand." This advice is particularly geared, quite strongly, toward self-published and independent writers.

Who started all this hype? And why are people buying into it? Tide® is a brand. Dove® is a brand. Coke® is a brand.

I am not laundry detergent. Or a bar of soap. Or a can of soda. I am a person. An individual, unique unto myself. And I expect to be treated as such.

Notice the trademark symbol? That denotes ownership. That is why products are branded. People should not be.

I am offended by all this "branding" talk along with "building a platform." Although "building a platform" makes some sort of sense. A platform is something upon which a person stands.

Fine. I stand on the platform of the underdog, the downtrodden, the overlooked, the ignored and the forgotten.

Has anyone seriously considered what it means to "brand?" It is a systematic way to force creative people to fit into cubbyholes: something that many creative people abhor but are told they must do in order to be successful. Apparently, individualism is a thing of the past.

I *revel* in my individuality. I **pride** myself on not being like everyone else. And I refuse to cater to current media and propaganda that tells me I must conform in order to succeed.

If you want to know who I am and what I'm all about, read my books and other writing. There's an awful lot of me in there. And, trust me, it's the best part of me. I'm not saying that to be egotistical. It is the one aspect of me I believe in, heart and soul. I can tell a good tale.

I believe in the possibility of a self-published author breaking free of this "brand" mold and being successful.

Look up the definition of brand because one of those definitions states that a brand is *any mark of disgrace; stigma.*

And everyone is so anxious to be branded.

Something else to think about: branding is for cattle. A brand is burned into the buttocks of cattle to signify ownership.

Which is exactly what all this branding nonsense is all about. Shuffling creative people around like cattle and placing them all into a corral. Better controlled and filed that way.

If you are comfortable with being branded, by all means, brand away. Links to articles about branding are listed under Helpful Links.

IF I MUST be "branded" brand me a rebel; unconventional; an outlaw.

Just don't burn that brand on my ass.

Where Do You Stand?

We are all apprentices in a craft where no one ever becomes a master. ~Ernest Hemingway

Something else contemporary independent authors are told they must have is a "platform."

A platform can be viewed as "something upon which a person stands."

Not quite as bad as branding; almost, but not quite. At least this makes sense.

Everyone believes in something. If they don't, they should. In the words of rock star John Mellencamp, "Ya gotta stand for something or you're gonna fall for anything."

I believe in freedom of speech. I believe in the freedom of religion and the freedom of choices. I believe in freedom of the press.

I stand upon the platform of the underdog, the downtrodden, the overlooked, the ignored and the forgotten.

Of course, it isn't that simple when it comes to building a writer's platform.

The writer's platform is more about your visibility than what you actually believe in. Your social media presence and interaction thereon, speaking engagements, who you know, what organizations you belong to and so on.

Set up a reading at your local library. Teach an elementary school class about writing. Contact local media for possible interviews about your book. Guest post on blogs and write articles related to a topic in your book, about writing in general or something you learned while writing your book. It's not only good exposure for your book it also helps to build your platform.

Just make certain it's a strong platform.

Luckily, articles abound on the Internet about how a writer can build a platform. I have included those links under Helpful Links.

Don't Marry a Genre
(You'll Have Really Funny-Looking Kids)

Don't classify me, read me. I'm a writer, not a genre.
~Carlos Fuentes

Genres are wonderful things. A book is categorized in a specific genre to help readers find what they seek.

They can also be traps.

Many authors write in only one genre. And that's fine. Writing in one specific genre earns readership and cultivates a following. It's customary for most writers to stick with one specific genre.

But what if you're writing in, say, the fantasy genre. And you get an idea for an action-thriller. Should you take the leap?

Why not? Your fantasy fans may not be thrilled with it, but you might gain a whole new audience.

If you do take that leap, expect some backlash from your fantasy fans. Family and friends. Readers and reviews. You'll get plenty of flack about it. But if it makes you happy, it's bound to make someone else happy.

Many authors write in different genres and are quite successful in both. For instance, James Rollins is best known for his Sigma Force series. But he also writes the Sanguine Series – a different spin on vampire lore – in collaboration with writer Rebecca Cantrell.

Even Dean Koontz has been known to step out of his genre. Though his genre is generally classified as suspense, when you begin subcategorizing each of his novels there is a vast array into which each one fits: thriller, spiritual, and action among them.

If you discard an idea simply because it doesn't fit into your specific "genre" you are denying – not only yourself and your creativity – you are also denying potential readers the benefit of your creativity.

~ 102 ~

If an idea comes knocking, you don't wanna knock it back; you want to answer the door and invite it in to sit a spell. See where it goes and what it's saying. Give it a chance to convince you of its viability. Then make the decision about whether or not you wish to pursue that idea and give it voice.

You're a writer. It's your job to explore many different avenues of writing.

You have nothing to lose by writing across genres, or by writing in many different genres.

And you never know what you might gain by doing so.

Bad Book Review? No Sweat

So what? All writers are lunatics! ~Cornelia Funke

No one is immune to a bad book review. So, at some point in your life, you're bound to get one. Or several.

Getting book reviews for your latest tome is important. It's also nice when they're positive; nicer still when they gush with praise.

But getting a negative book review is considered a stumbling block; a "black mark" if you will.

First of all, don't allow the negatives to get to you. It is the opinion of only one person. You'll never know why she or he really didn't like your book. You can only read what was written about it.

Instead of seeing that negative review as a stumbling block, look at it as a stepping stone.

Was the criticism constructive? Were there any points made that you should seriously consider? Was any aspect of the criticism helpful?

For instance, "didn't like the characters" is vague and not useful. But something like, "Sally was weak and a whiner; she didn't measure up to the hero's image at all," is more specific. It tells you that you may need to work on those characters. It could also tell you that the reader missed the point of the character but it isn't your job to explain that.

My favorite negative response is, "Too wordy, too long."

Admittedly, my initial response to this is akin to Mozart's in *Amadeus*: I use exactly the number of words required, no more, no less. But that is my writer's ego talking.

But part of me agrees with this. I love words. I love the works of Dean Koontz and Stephen King, both authors who weave words very well. And perhaps, subconsciously, I attempt to emulate them. But I also realize that I need to work on writing more succinctly. I need to be more aware of the words I use and do some "tightening up" especially when it comes to descriptions.

Most reviews will be more general in nature and rarely be specific. Most people who read the book know only that she or he likes it or doesn't like it. And that may be all the review says.

Objectivity is the key in reading book reviews. The reviewer isn't reading the book as you wrote it. Each person is reading from her or his own perspective which will be different from your own. Since each reviewer did not write the book, none of them will have the "inside scoop" on what is vital to the story. You present them with the story and it is up to the individual to take from it what she or he deems vital.

It may have been important for you to create Sally as a whiner. Apparently that didn't appeal to that one reader. And that's okay. It does not reflect negatively on the reader or on you. It merely means that character didn't appeal to this reader. And there's nothing wrong with that. Just like every person you meet isn't going to be a person you like, so every reader isn't going to like all your characters.

Responding to book reviews, whether good or bad, is never a good idea. Those responses could come back one day to bite you in the derriere whether they were good responses or not.

And responding to a negative book review in an attempt to justify your writing is in poor taste. It undermines your confidence in yourself as a writer. Even if the reviewer attacks you on a personal level, let it go. It isn't worth getting entangled in verbal jousting with someone whom you've never met. And continued contact with someone, especially in this day and age, could very well result in an unwanted meeting.

Take the bad book reviews with the good. And celebrate that you have book reviews.

This article first appeared on Closed the Cover:
www.closedthecover.com

Fun Stuff

I love deadlines. I love the whooshing noise they make as they go by. ~Douglas Adams

Writing the Demons Away

The purpose of a writer is to keep civilization from destroying itself. ~Albert Camus

If you've ever watched *The Twilight Zone* (1985) there was one episode particularly poignant to writers.

Personal Demons was a story about a man who was a writer. A writing man, you could say. He found himself plagued by these little hooded creatures. They followed him everywhere, creating chaos and mayhem along the way. He tried to talk about these creatures with other people but, of course, no one could see them except him.

One day he looked up and there were those creatures standing around him looking at him. He asked them "What do I have to do to get rid of you?"

One of the little demons stepped forward and said, "Write about us and you'll never see us again."

That's how it is when a writer first gets a glimpse of an idea. It begins as a thought. That's all, just a thought. It begins to build. Characters show up who act out what you're thinking. Next thing you know, those characters invade your life.

It's like having a bunch of little creatures follow you everywhere, wrecking your thought processes, interfering with everyday tasks, sometimes even influencing how you act and interact with other people.

It isn't until the writer begins the actual writing process that the characters settle down. Once those characters come to life upon the page, they're still with you, every day and in every step you take. But they're not clamoring for your attention because they have that now.

I suppose, in a way, a writer can think of it as a birthing process. The characters creating their mayhem are contractions. Putting them on paper is giving them life.

It may seem a bit on the macabre side but it's part of the creative process. *Personal Demons* illustrates it in a total of twelve minutes, presenting it as an almost frightening experience.

It can be a little frightening. Until the writer learns and understands that she or he must write these characters into being, must breathe life into them so that others can experience them as well.

That's all characters, ideas and stories want: to be given life.
Watch *Personal Demons* on YouTube.

Personal Demons, Season 1 Episode 44:
http://bit.ly/1mAd2B3

How Characters Act

Cats are dangerous companions for writers because cat watching is a near-perfect method of writing avoidance. ~Dan Greenburg

Do you visualize what your characters do as you write about them? Do you change how they act as you are writing?

On the lighter side of writing, The Playwright, a sketch performed on The Carol Burnett Show, exemplifies what it looks like when a writer writes. It is a hilarious glimpse into the mind of the writer.

As Harvey Korman writes in the background, Carol and the gang act out exactly what Harvey writes. They acclimate themselves to several plot changes and pre-act on actions when Harvey hesitates. In less than six minutes, the viewer sees what the writer and the writer's characters go through during a writing session.

It is a wonderful display of the writing process. It is a comedic look at how the imagination and creativity that goes into writing a particular scene and how the characters may feel about that.

Characters have feelings? Of course they do. As the writer, it is your job to incorporate those feelings into them so that your reader may feel something as well.

Characters also have a way of doing their own thing. Which is not bad. It can sometimes lead you in new directions or give you new ideas about the story you're writing.

But the next time you're working on a writing project, picture in your mind how your characters are acting out what you write. It might make you a smile.

Oh, and if you must take aspirin during the writing process, do give the characters a heads-up.

Watch The Playwright on YouTube:
http://bit.ly/1fxtzhy

Create a Book Trailer for Under $50

Find out the reason that commands you to write; see whether it has spread its roots into the very depth of your heart; confess to yourself you would have to die if you were forbidden to write.
~Rainer Maria Rilke

Book Trailers are a valuable marketing tool, especially for self-published and independent writers. Creating your own book trailer doesn't have to be expensive.

I recently got burned when I hired someone to create a book trailer for me. I ordered and paid for the trailer in February, 2014. As of this publication I have not received the book trailer and repeated contact with the woman goes unacknowledged. Even though she has a lot of Internet presence, I doubt I will ever hear from her or receive a book trailer and I'm out the money I sent her.

That said, I decided to create my own. *Why didn't you just do that to begin with?* you may ask. Quite honestly, I wasn't confident in my ability to make one and to make it look professional. I am the world's biggest techno-clod and did not believe in my own capabilities. That, and try finding an image of a gold sword that can be used and doesn't cost an arm and a leg.

Once I decided to create my own book trailer I was delighted to learn a great many things, including the fact that I am perfectly capable of producing something aesthetically appealing as well as a video which presents my book in a professional light. Allow me to take you step by step through the process I used to create my book trailer.

CONTENT

Make a list of about a half-dozen to a dozen highlights from your book. Use a few words to get big ideas across. This will help strengthen your writing as well as force you to seriously contemplate the most important aspects of your book.

I created a total of ten highlights of my novel for my trailer. Here are three very important aspects of the Sword of Tilk Book One: Worlds Apart:

Barbara Neely wakes up one morning in a different world
She must wield the golden Sword of Tilk to defeat Balfourant, enemy of the Realm
When Balfourant kidnaps her daughter, Barbara must conquer her own demons to save her

I broke down the aspects even further and added a few more relevant highlights to tell the reader a little more about what Barbara experiences.

IMAGES

While you are making that list of your book's highlights, consider images you would like to use to enhance those highlights.

If you are artistic you can create the images yourself with artwork or photography. If you're like me, you may need to scour the Internet in search of images that are copyright free, royalty free and not too costly.

Two websites offer royalty/copyright free images for unlimited use: www.morguefile.com and www.pixabay.com. Both sites have a large selection of images; however, their selection can sometimes be limited in scope.

Wikicommons (www.commons.wikimedia.org) is also a source for free images as long as you stick with images in public domain. That way you don't have to worry about licensing, sharing and the like.

Three top websites with images for use are Dreamstime (www.dreamstime.com), IStock (www.istockphoto.com) and Shutterstock (www.shutterstock.com). These images are at a price. All three sites have two different ways to pay: 1) Purchase credits or 2) Subscription. Each photo on the sites is worth a certain number of credits. By purchasing the credits you then get an image and the credits it is worth is deducted from your purchased credits. Purchase a subscription and you are allowed to download a certain number of images within a specific time period.

I suggest going with Dreamstime which is where I was finally able to find an image of a gold sword. The cost is $39 for 5 images within a one-week time period and this is the best deal if you only need a few images. I was able to find five images which I felt were appropriate for my trailer.

PUTTING IT TOGETHER

If you have Windows on your computer (who doesn't?) then you have Windows Live Movie Maker. It's actually a fun little program to play with.

Begin by uploading just a few images and text. Each time you need to add a new frame, click on *Title* in the tool bar. To add images, click on *Add videos and photo*. Once you have added the photo, click on *Caption* to add text.

Now you get to have some fun.

For the images, click on *Animations*. This will give you a selection of "special effects" for your image. Dissolves, transitions, patterns and reveals are just a few of the effects you can add to each of your images. Also under *Animations* you'll find Pan and Zoom to further enhance your images. Both can be combined to really make your image pop. Be aware, however, that not all Animation choices will be available for the very first frame of your movie. I believe the program assumes the first frame is the title frame and effects for that particular frame are limited.

Text can also be manipulated by clicking on *Text Tools*. You can scroll it, zoom it, swing it or fly it. Try different combinations to see which text effect works best with the animations on your images. Don't be afraid to experiment. You might be surprised at what you come up with.

SOUNDTRACK

A book trailer is nothing without the proper musical accompaniment. Again, if you are capable of creating your own music or have a friend who can do that for you, by all means create away. One more aspect of your creativity you can display is always a good thing.

There are quite a few free music websites out there but the trouble is the selection is limited. I have yet to find truly "free" music which would serve as good accompaniment to my trailers. I used Melody Loops (www.melodyloops.com). Most of the music they have available only costs $10 which isn't much if you think about it. They have a huge variety of music which you can use as you wish and you can give it a listen before you buy. The site also allows you to "loop" the musical selection so it will match the length of your video. Or you can choose "Fit to music" in your Windows Live Movie Maker (under the Project tab) so the video matches the length of the music. When you download the music, be sure to save it in a place where it is easily accessible.

Here is the really tricky part: sometimes the music doesn't work well with the video. It's a good idea to download Freemake Audio Converter (www.freemake.com/free_audio_converter/ - it's FREE) and convert those music files to mp3 or wav. Try each one because the wav worked best for mine. Even if the original file is already in mp3 use the converter and convert it to mp3. This works out any glitches in the download and the music flows more smoothly. Using the original file without converting it through Freemake sometimes causes the track to "break" in places it isn't supposed to break.

Click *Add Music* on the Home tab and select the music file. Click *Fit to Music* if the soundtrack runs short or long. This will increase or decrease the amount of time each frame slides by so the music and images coincide.

REVIEW YOUR VIDEO

Watch your completed video. Several times. Watch your pans, zooms, and transitions closely to make sure they flow smoothly. Read your text and then read it again to catch any errors and to be certain it is coherent. Watch both the images and the text until you are confident they work well together and present your book in its best light.

THE MATH

Let's do the math: $39 for images (which works out to a little less than $8 per image), $10 for music. That's a total of $49 to create my own book trailer. That is about one-fourth of what I paid to have one created and a fraction of the cost of most trailer production sites I have visited.

If you use your own images and music, it pretty much won't cost you a thing. That's even better than $49!

A FEW EXTRA TIDBITS

Now that your book trailer is complete you'll want to upload it to YouTube, Vimeo, Goodreads and any other sites which will allow you to upload it. Before you do, you must save it in the proper format.

To do this, click on the icon in the upper left corner of the Movie Maker screen. Choose "Save Movie" and "Recommended for this Project" at the very top of the choice list. Save it in a location where it is easily accessible. You are now ready to upload your video. Be forewarned: it takes forever for the video to upload. So once you click the "upload" button on the site you're uploading to you can pretty much start a load of laundry, clean your bathroom, brush your teeth and get dinner started before it is completed. You could probably color your hair and wash the dog while you're at it.

Also, when you add a frame in Movie Maker by clicking on *Title* in the tool bar, don't be surprised if the frame appears prior to a frame you've just created. For some reason, that's how it works. You may also encounter some extra blank frames tossed in. Delete the frames you don't need and move the frames around in the order you want them to appear.

Keep the trailer short and sweet. Ninety minutes is probably the max you'll want to do for a book trailer. If you're doing a trailer with a more poignant or specific message, two minutes, tops.

If a techno-clod like me can create my own book trailer, anyone can. Save yourself time, money and lots of aggravation by giving it a try.

The videos I have created aren't bad. My ideal would be to have them actually filmed but film costs are far and beyond my budget. Check out the links below to see each video:

Sword of Tilk Book One: Worlds Apart
http://youtu.be/uxTa6cIrteI

A Final Word (In a Manner of Speaking)

If my doctor told me I had only six minutes to live, I wouldn't brood. I'd type a little faster. ~Isaac Asimov

Dying to be a Writer? Well, not exactly

It is one thing to claim "When it's my time, I'm ready to go!"

It is most decidedly, most definitely, a completely different matter when that moment is staring you in the face.

I spent seven months writing the *Sword of Tilk Trilogy*. Another five months spent proofreading, editing and rewriting. Finally, I reached the point where it was time to let go: it was time to publish the trilogy and allow it to stand on its own.

I decided to try and publish all three books on June 12, 2013. It was the anniversary date of the day I began writing the books. I thought it would be neat to publish on that date.

As it turned out, I didn't feel well that day. I had taken that day off from work for the express purpose of publishing the books via createspace.com. All I could do was work on them piecemeal to complete some of the details required to get them to final publication.

I missed the self-imposed deadline and decided to aim for June 14th which was my father's birthday.

I felt absolutely horrible. There was a pain in my shoulder that wouldn't go away. I figured it was a pulled muscle. Then I contracted what I thought was bronchitis. I've had bronchitis before. About the only thing to be done for it is lots of sleep, lots of fluids and plenty of over-the-counter meds. I couldn't see a doctor at that point but that's another story.

I couldn't get to work for feeling so bad. But so determined was I to get those three books published that I intermittently worked on them; there simply is no daunting the creative spirit.

I finally managed to get all three books copyrighted on the 14th and the official publication date is the 16th – Father's Day. We used to tease Daddy a lot about his birthday and Father's day oftentimes falling so closely together. We always treated them separately – they were two different days after all – regardless of how much grumbling Daddy did about that.

Once the books passed the review process, I ordered review copies on the 18th. I felt somewhat better and was ready to return to work the next day. There was nothing more I could do with the books: a careful once-over when the copies arrived and I could then put them out there for sale on Amazon.com.

All was right with the world.

I settled in to relax and watch a little television until it was bedtime.

It happened around eight o'clock.

I couldn't breathe. Short, almost painful puffs of air were all I could do. It felt like drowning. It felt like suffocating. Even thinking about it sends surges of fear and panic through my veins.

And there it was: this could possibly be *that moment*.

That realization brought an entire barrage of emotions to the surface, the foremost of those being the truth: I'm not ready.

For all my talk, I wasn't ready.

Or maybe a little voice told me it wasn't my time.

Whatever the reason, I chose to get help rather than to wait and allow the fates to determine my demise.

As it all turned out, I had been walking around for about a week with pneumonia. But it was the heart attack that triggered the difficulty to breathe.

One wiseacre (who shall remain nameless but she knows who she is) asked me if I "heard the angels sing" as in some people see their lives flash before their eyes and some people hear the angels sing before they die. I responded with," No, I didn't hear the angels sing, but I didn't hear no devil laughin', neither."

I find a certain irony in the fact that this all occurred within hours of my ordering proof copies of the trilogy. Was there some significance to the fact that it happened after I had everything all finished and published? Was there a message to be found in the fact that I had yet to see a finished copy of the books? Like maybe

I should stop procrastinating so much and get on the stick and get my work out there?

Or maybe the incentive was in wanting to see the finished products, to hold them in my hands.

I don't know, really. The Universe speaks in symbols rather than in plain English and I've never been very good at interpreting symbolism.

And I would like to clarify that the books weren't what led to the heart attack. Writing gives me great joy and pleasure, even more once I hold the finished product in my hand.

No, I have to admit it was my own doing. A lifetime of bad eating habits, even more poor exercise habits and not keeping track of my blood sugar.

But all that is changing.

I take this as a new lease, a second chance and about a dozen other clichés appropriate for the experience. It is definitely a prime opportunity to put priorities in order and realize what is really important in this life.

With that in mind, I have a lot of writing to do.

Helpful Links

Rereading a good book is like visiting a wonderful and trusted friend. ~ Pen

There are, literally, millions of articles on the Internet in regards to writing and self-publishing. These are but a few that I found helpful.

How to Make your own book covers in MS Word
http://bit.ly/VVoNHe

This article explains very well the difference between Vanity, Subsidy and Self-Publishing
VanitySubsidy Publishers
http://bit.ly/1qMUH4Q

How to be media friendly to sell more books
http://bit.ly/1wOM8vn

Branding

Personal Branding 101
http://onforb.es/VVNuDe

How To Brand Yourself
http://bit.ly/1thIjwq

How To Brand Yourself: An Introduction
http://bit.ly/XZ1xtH

Platform

101 Quick Actions You Can Take Today to Build the Writer Platform of Your Dreams
http://bit.ly/VTgVGs

The Basics of Building a Writer's Platform
http://bit.ly/1osPBFI

What is a Writer's Platform?
http://abt.cm/1tTyO4c

4 Keys to Building a Writer's Platform
http://bit.ly/1lAc9d5

The "New Author Platform" - What writers need to know
http://onforb.es/1qnQvHK

Speaking Engagements

How to get Your First Speaking Engagement in Just 3 Weeks
http://bit.ly/1n4Eeo6

17 Ways to Find Speaking Opportunities
http://bit.ly/1wOMbr4

How to Get More Speaking Gigs: Don't Wait for Opportunities, Create Them
http://huff.to/1qNWDGH

Writing Stuff of Interest

Savvy Writers
A plethora of writing articles
http://savvybookwriters.wordpress.com/

Closed the Cover
Opportunities for guest blogging and signing up for book tours
www.closedthecover.com

A Writer's Journey
Nat Russo
Good, solid writing advice with a great sense of humor
http://bit.ly/1tUYM8o

From the Author

If every person in the world planted a seed of hope, and if every one of those seeds grew, there would not be enough room in the world for hate. ~Pen

Writing is hope.

If you have ever read something that you wanted to share with the world because you felt the world needed to read it; read something that touched you in some way, brought a tear to your eye or tugged at your heart, then you know the above statement is true.

Changing the world may be outside the writer's purview but something which instills hope is one of the writer's many talents and true assets. Words have the capability of changing perspectives and opinions, opening a heart or a mind, creating ideas and visions for the future.

That's an awful lot of power in the hands of the writer.

Use it wisely.

About the Author

Bitten by the writing bug at the age of ten, Pen is an avid reader in addition to being a prolific writer. A native Georgian she lived in Hollywood, California for a year and a half (pursuing Film Studies – an interesting distraction) and six weeks in Asheville, NC (attempting to get herself together).

Influenced by the world around her, Pen writes whatever comes into her fuzzy little red head (currently Vidal Sassoon Merlot Vibrant Red). She writes in no specific genre as she has a variety of interests and passions about which to write.

In addition to reading and writing, Pen loves movies and music, particularly the music of the 80s and prior. Again, her passions for movies and music are as eclectic as her writing and reading.

Not a huge fan of television she is, nonetheless, currently an avid follower of ABC's *Once Upon A Time* television series. So much so, that this series inspired her to write the *Sword of Tilk* Trilogy and influenced the writing of *Nero's Fiddle*, though it is hardly recognizable in any of those tomes.

Pen enjoys reading the works of Edgar Allan Poe, Agatha Christie, Dean Koontz, Stephen King, James Rollins' Sigma Force series, Lindsay Buroker, Kathryn Harvey and Judy Mercer (may she rest in peace). A host of other authors grace her bookshelves, too numerous to mention. She has been known to reread books numerous times. Rereading a good book is like visiting a wonderful and trusted friend.

Pen currently resides in the Atlanta, Georgia area where she is staff to two felines.

She may be contacted via the contact form on her website www.penspen.info.

Other books by Pen

Sword of Tilk Book One: Worlds Apart
Sword of Tilk Book Two: Strange Land
Sword of Tilk Book Three: At Sword's End
9.5B
Return Me
Wisdom
Hope
Faith
Train Ride (and other Chilling Tales)
I AM
God is Praying
An Introduction to Maladaptive Daydreaming
Christmas Blessings
Lifelines: Things to Hold On To
Nero's Fiddle – due out October 2014

www.penspen.info

Pen's Amazon Author Page
http://www.amazon.com/author/pen

Merchandise
www.cafepress.com/penspen

Smashwords
http://bit.ly/WDQRAg

You may also follow Pen on these Social Media sites:

Facebook
http://on.fb.me/1mVmJt4

Twitter
@penspen

Goodreads
http://bit.ly/1tSrw3V

Or follow her blogs

Wordpress

Pen's Pen
http://bit.ly/1nbIIO0

The Muse Speaketh
http://bit.ly/1nxtc9z

www.ingramcontent.com/pod-product-compliance
Lightning Source LLC
Chambersburg PA
CBHW070147290526
45789CB00002B/671